中英文版高速铁路运营管理系列教材
Chinese-English High Speed Railway Operation
Management Coursebook Series

高速铁路客运服务

HIGH SPEED RAILWAY PASSENGER SERVICE

主　编　李云飞　刘鸿婷
副主编　杨图南　张雯雯　赵力耀　李精忠　张世涛　唐　丽
翻　译　王艳苹

云南出版集团
云南人民出版社

图书在版编目（CIP）数据

高速铁路客运服务 / 李云飞, 刘鸿婷主编; 王艳苹翻译. -- 昆明: 云南人民出版社, 2020.12
中英文版高速铁路运营管理系列教材
ISBN 978-7-222-19549-3

Ⅰ.①高… Ⅱ.①李…②刘…③王… Ⅲ.①高速铁路—铁路运输—客运服务—高等职业教育—教材—汉、英 Ⅳ.①U293.3

中国版本图书馆CIP数据核字(2020)第251530号

出 品 人：	赵石定
责任编辑：	冯 琰
助理编辑：	谢筑娟
封面设计：	张益珲
责任校对：	胡元青
责任印制：	马文杰

高速铁路客运服务
GAOSU TIELU KEYUN FUWU

主 编：	李云飞	刘鸿婷	
副主编：	杨图南	张雯雯	赵力耀
	李精忠	张世涛	唐 丽
翻 译：	王艳苹		

出 版	云南出版集团 云南人民出版社
发 行	云南人民出版社
社 址	昆明市环城西路609号
邮 编	650034
网 址	www.ynpph.com.cn
E-mail	ynrms@sina.com
开 本	787mm×1092mm 1/16
印 张	16.5
字 数	301千
版 次	2020年12月第1版第1次印刷
印 刷	云南金伦云印实业股份有限公司
书 号	ISBN 978-7-222-19549-3
定 价	42.00元

云南人民出版社微信公众号

如需购买图书、反馈意见，请与我社联系
总编室：0871-64109126　发行部：0871-64108507　审校部：0871-64164626　印制部：0871-64191534

版权所有　侵权必究　印装差错　负责调换

前 言

Preface

《高速铁路客运服务》采用中英文对照排版模式，为中外读者深入解读了高铁车站内及列车上的基本服务知识。教材本着促进职业教育科学化、标准化、规范化的原则，运用创新的教学方法，设置了项目、任务、模块等教学单元，具有非常强的操作性、指导性和实用性。教材中的项目包括学前准备、课堂学习、课堂练习、课后拓展4个模块，学中做、做中学，能充分调动教师教学能动性，丰富教师课堂教学内容形式，激发学生学习主动性。

本教材囊括了高速铁路客运服务的基本内容、要求，以及旅客采用高铁出行涉及的各环节服务细节，具体分为8个项目28个任务。主要内容包括：项目一高速铁路客运服务概述、项目二高速铁路客运服务礼仪、项目三售票作业、项目四高速铁路车站进站服务、项目五高速铁路车站站台乘降服务、项目六高速铁路车站出站服务、项目七高速铁路乘务服务、项目八重点旅客服务。

本教材由云南交通职业技术学院李

High Speed Railway Passenger Service is English-Chinese typesetting for domestic and overseas readers to deeply understand the basic service content in high speed railway stations and trains. The coursebook is compiled with innovative teaching method and has the teaching units of project, task, module and so on, and is based on the principle of scientific, standard and normalized vocational education. The coursebook is highly operational, instructive and practical. Each project in the coursebook includes four modules of Preparation before Class, In-class Learning, In-class exercise and After-class Activity. The mode of "practice during learning and learning through practice" will highly motivate teachers, enrich teaching content and forms and greatly inspire students.

The coursebook includes the basic content and requirements of high speed railway passenger service, as well as detailed service in all parts of high speed railway transportation with 8 projects and 28 tasks. The major contents are: Project 1 Overview of High Speed Railway Passenger Service, Project 2 High Speed Railway Passenger Service Etiquette, Project 3 Ticket Selling, Project 4 High Speed Railway Check-in Service, Project 5 High Speed Railway Station Platform Elevator Service,

云飞、刘鸿婷主编并统稿，负责编写的老师有杨图南、张雯雯、赵力耀、李精忠、张世涛、唐丽等。英文翻译得到了云南大学赵斌教授的大力支持，王艳苹老师主要负责英文翻译。在本教材编写过程中，参考了许多专家的研究成果和有关文献资料，在此谨向各位专家、作者表示衷心的感谢。

由于编者水平有限，书中难免有疏漏之处，敬请广大读者谅解，真诚期待读者和同行多提宝贵意见。

编 者

2020 年 5 月

Project 6 High Speed Railway Station Check-out Service, Project 7 High Speed Railway Passenger Service and Project 8 Service to Special Passengers.

  The coursebook was chiefly compiled and edited by Li Yunfei and Liu Hongting of Yunnan Jiaotong College, and Yang Tunan, Zhang Wenwen, Zhao Liyao, Li Jingzhong, Zhang Shitao and Tang Li took part in the compilation of the coursebook. Professor Zhao Bin of Yunnan University greatly supported the translation and the book and Wang Yanping was in charge of the translation. In the process of compilation, research and documents of many experts were also referred to, and we wish to express our heartfelt thanks to the experts and authors.

  Due to the limited knowledge of the editors, there may be inevitable omissions in the book, we expect the understanding of readers and sincerely look forward to the valuable suggestions from readers and peers.

Editor

May 2020

目 录

项目一　高速铁路客运服务概述
Project 1　Overview of High Speed Railway Passenger Service

任务一　高速铁路客运内容概述 ··· 1

Task 1　Overview of High Speed Railway Passenger Service Content ············ 1

任务二　高速铁路客运服务概述 ··· 10

Task 2　Overview of High Speed Railway Passenger Service ························ 10

项目二　高速铁路客运服务礼仪
Project 2　High Speed Railway Passenger Service Etiquette

任务一　礼仪概述 ·· 19

Task 1　Etiquette Overview ··· 19

任务二　高速铁路客运服务仪容仪表礼仪 ·· 27

Task 2　High Speed Railway Passenger Service Appearance Etiquette ············ 27

任务三　高速铁路客运服务仪态礼仪 ··· 36

Task 3　High Speed Railway Passenger Service Manners and Etiquette ·········· 36

任务四　高速铁路客运服务语言礼仪 ··· 56

Task 4　Language Etiquette of High Speed Railway Passenger Service ··········· 56

任务五　高速铁路客运涉外礼仪 ··· 64

Task 5　High Speed Railway Passenger Service Foreign-related Etiquette ······· 64

项目三 售票作业
Project 3　Ticket Selling

任务一　车票认知 ··· 77
Task 1　Recognize Train Ticket ·· 77

任务二　窗口人工售票 ··· 86
Task 2　Manual Ticket Selling at the Ticket Office ···························· 86

任务三　自助售票 ··· 97
Task 3　Self-service Ticket Vending ·· 97

项目四　高速铁路车站进站服务
Project 4　High Speed Railway Check-in Service

任务一　安检服务 ··· 114
Task 1　Security Check Service ·· 114

任务二　检票服务 ··· 124
Task 2　Check-in Service ·· 124

任务三　候车服务 ··· 133
Task 3　Waiting Service ·· 133

项目五　高速铁路车站站台乘降服务
Project 5　High Speed Railway Station Platform Elevator Service

任务一　站台概述 ··· 139
Task 1　Overview of Platform ·· 139

任务二　站台客运员工作概述 ·· 145
Task 2　Job Description of Platform Passenger Service Employees ········ 145

任务三 乘降服务与站车交接 ·150

Task 3 Elevating Service, Station and Train Handover ·150

项目六 高速铁路车站出站服务
Project 6　High Speed Railway Station Check-out Service

任务一 出站检票作业 ·156

Task 1 Check out ·156

任务二 违章乘车的处理 ·163

Task 2 Processing of Illegal Boarding ·163

任务三 违章携带物品的处理 ·171

Task 3 Deal with Illegal Luggage ·171

任务四 车票、证件丢失的处理 ·178

Task 4 Dealing with Loss of Ticket or Certificate ·178

任务五 误售、误购、误乘、坐过站的处理 ·186

Task 5 Dealing with Mistaken Selling&Buying of Ticket, Mistaking and Missing Stop ·186

项目七 高速铁路乘务服务
Project 7　High Speed Railway Passenger Service

任务一 乘务组组成与人员要求 ·191

Task 1 Composition and Requirement of Train Attendants ·191

任务二 主要乘务人员岗位职责 ·199

Task 2 Job Description of Major Crew Members ·199

任务三 乘务工作服务流程 ·207

Task 3 Passenger Service Procedure ·207

任务四　动车组突发情况处理···218
Task 4　Emergency Handling in CHR Trains·································218

项目八　重点旅客服务
Project 8　Service to Special Passengers

任务一　外籍旅客服务···230
Task 1　Service to Foreign Passengers······································230

任务二　重点旅客服务···237
Task 2　Service to Special Passengers······································237

任务三　列车接待工作···247
Task 3　Reception in the Train··247

参考文献··256
Reference··256

项目一　高速铁路客运服务概述

Project 1　Overview of High Speed Railway Passenger Service

任务一　高速铁路客运内容概述

Task 1　Overview of High Speed Railway Passenger Service Content

模块一　学前准备

Module 1　Preparation before Class

请上网查阅国内高铁的情况，简略地做一个总结。

Search information about high speed railways in China on the Internet and make a summary.

课前学习笔记
Study Notes before Class

模块二　课堂学习

知识点一：高速铁路客运工作的基本要求

1. 保证运输安全

保证安全是铁路运输最重要的任务，为此，要切实遵守各项安全制度，维护运输秩序，确保铁路旅客运输的安全。众所周知，整个运输生产过程，是众人的联合劳动，在生产实践和作业过程中具有高度的连续性、联动性和准确性。在这种联合劳动中，哪怕有一个环节、一道工序出现纰漏，都可能导致车毁人亡、运输中断。安全是铁路运输这个大系统得以稳定、正常运作的必要条件。为了确保安全，必须教育每个铁路职工发扬人民铁路为人民的光荣传统，遵纲守纪，顾全大局，在任何情况下都把保证铁路畅通、安全作为自己的职责；维护好站车秩序，做好危险物品的查堵工作，并对所有用于旅客运输的设备定期检查、维修，确保旅客出行安全。高速铁路客运安全要着眼于避免旅客列车事故，使高速列车平安进、出站，安全过区间。

2. 提高旅客列车运行速度

提高旅客列车运行速度是提高客运服务质量的重要方面之一，是铁路发展

Module 2　In-class Study

Key Point 1: Basic Requirement for High Speed Railway Passenger Service

1. Ensure Transportation Safety

The most important task of railway transportation is to ensure safety, thus, it is significant to safety regulations and safeguard transportation order to ensure the safety of passenger service. It is known to all that the entire transportation process is the joint work of all requiring high continuity, linkage and precision. In the process of the joint work, any flaw in the process will lead to rash or transportation interruption. Safety is necessary for the stable and normal running of the railway transportation. Therefore, it is necessary to teach each railway employee to carry forward the tradition of serving the people, abiding by the rules and bearing in mind the overall interests to take the responsibility of ensuring the smooth running and safety of railway. It is the employees' duty to keep order at the stations, to check and block dangerous items and check, repair transportation devices regularly to ensure safety. The key point of high speed railway passenger service is to avoid train accident, to ensure the safe entering and exit of train and safe passing through sections.

2. Speeding up Passenger Train

Speeding up train is an important part in enhancing passenger service quality, and it is also the main trend of railway development and the urge of the passengers. With the development of our country's social economy,

的大趋势，也是广大旅客的迫切要求。随着我国社会经济的发展和人民生活水平的提高及生活节奏的加快，人们的时间观念越来越强。速度成了选择交通方式的重要指标，它将是今后不同客运交通方式在竞争中成败的关键。提高列车运行速度也是有效地加速机车车辆周转、提高运输能力和降低运输成本的重要手段。

3. 加强运输计划的编制，组织旅客有序流动

有计划地组织旅客运输，是保证完成旅客运输任务的基础，要经济合理地使用机车车辆和其他技术设备，安全正点地完成运输工作。必须在客流调查的基础上，正确编制旅客运输计划，组织均衡运输。要加强对客流信息的了解、掌握、传递、反馈、处理，把客票销售计划和运能安排紧密结合起来。对主要客运大站和重点车次，每日要进行客流分析，及时掌握客流变化情况，了解客流的构成、特点及其波动性，用科学的市场预测方法对不同时期的客流情况进行预测和分析，提高计划编制的科学性和准确性。

4. 提高服务质量，营造舒适的旅行环境

服务质量的优劣直接影响到铁路运

people's living standard is improved. People's concept of time is becoming stronger and speed is a significant factor in choosing means of travelling and it is also the key to success in the competition of the means of passenger transportation. Speeding up trains is also an important way to accelerate turnover, improve transporting capacity and lower cost.

3. Enhancing Transportation Plan Making and Organizing Orderly Flow of Passengers

Orderly organization of passenger transportation is the basis for the completion of passenger transportation, it is necessary to use trains and other equipment economically and reasonably to complete transportation safely and punctually. Accurate passenger transportation plan making to organize balanced transportation shall be conducted on the basis of passenger flow survey. It is required to better understand, command, transmit, feedback and process passenger flow information and to combine ticket selling plan and transportation capacity arrangement. Daily passenger flow analysis in major stations and important trains is required to know passenger flow change, structure, feature and its fluctuation, therefore, predication and analysis of passenger flow in different periods can be done in a scientific market predication way to enhance scientificity and accuracy of plan making.

4. Enhancing Service Quality to Create a Comfortable Travelling Environment

Quality of service directly influences

输企业的生命力,优质服务是高速铁路进入市场的"入场券"。服务观念不仅是一个经济观念,更是一个重要的文化观念。优质服务能够增加运输产品的文化含量,增加产品的文化附加值和企业形象的附加值,满足旅客的精神需要。通过优质服务与旅客进行情感和心理的沟通,是吸引旅客、开拓市场的有效手段,为此,要强化客运队伍的培训,使服务操作规范化、上水平,对客运员工要实行优胜劣汰、竞争上岗的制度,要求全体客运员工努力工作,将站、车建设成为一个温馨的"旅客之家"。

知识点二:高速铁路基层客运工作的内容及岗位设置

高速铁路客运部门要加强人才队伍建设,实施人才强路战略,紧紧抓住培养、吸引和用好人才三个环节,以经营管理人才、专业技术人才、技能人才三支队伍建设为重点,构建多层次、多渠道的教育培训体系,形成完善的高速铁路客运人才培训、选拔任用、考核评价、激励保障和合理流动机制,造就高素质的高速铁路客运人才队伍。

高速铁路客运工作是高速铁路运输生产中的重要组成部分,随着近些年来旅客列车的提速、多条高速铁路线路的开通运营,铁路客运业务的增长非常迅

vitality of rail transportation enterprises, therefore, high quality service is the admission ticket for high speed railways entering the market. Concept of service is not only an economic concept but also a cultural concept. Quality service can increase cultural content in transportation, added cultural value in product and enterprise image to satisfy the spiritual need of passengers. It is effective to attract travelers and expand market through quality service and communicate with travelers emotionally and psychologically. Therefore, it is required to train the transportation team in terms of standard and capable operation through survival of the fittest and competition system to make the stations and trains a cozy home for passengers through hard work of all employees.

Key Point 2: Content and Post Setting in High Speed Railway Grass-root Passenger Service

It is significant for high speed railway passenger service department to enhance talents team building to cultivate, attract and use talents with "strengthening railways through talents" strategy. With the key construction of operation talents, professional personnel and skilled talents, a multilevel and multiple channel educating and training system is to be built to form a complete system for talent training, selection, evaluation, encouragement and reasonable flow for building high quality high speed railway passenger service talents.

Passenger service is an important component in high speed railway transportation.

速。高速铁路旅客运输过程是一个多部门、多岗位相互协调和联动的过程，车站和列车作为铁路客运的主要部门在客运服务方面扮演着重要的角色。高速铁路客运基层岗位的设置与高速铁路旅客运输的基本作业流程相关。高速铁路旅客运输的基本作业流程如图1-1所示。

Passenger service increases rapidly with the speeding up of passenger trains and operation of many high speed railways in recent years. High speed railway passenger service is a coordinated and interconnected process involving multiple departments and positions, in the process, stations and trains play a significant part as the major department. Grass-root post setting is relevant to the basic operation procedure in passenger service. The basic operation procedure in passenger service is illustrated in Figure 1-1.

发送作业：sending operation　　途中作业：en-route operation　　达到作业：arrival operation

图 1-1　高速铁路旅客运输的基本作业流程

Figure 1-1　Basic Operation Procedure in High Speed Railway Passenger Service

（1）发送作业包括：问询、售票、候车室服务、检票、上车作业。

（2）途中作业包括：中转签证、列车服务工作等。

（3）到达作业包括：下车作业、验票。

以上的作业内容由许多不同岗位的客运人员来完成，主要包括基层的操作岗位和管理岗位，高速铁路客运基层岗位结构如图1-2所示。

（1）Sending operation: inquiry, ticket selling, waiting room service, check-in, boarding.

（2）En-route operation: transfer entry visa, train service and so on.

（3）Arrival operation: getting off, ticket check.

The above-mentioned content is completed by employees of different posts, mainly including grass-root operating and management posts. High speed railway passenger service grass-root posts are illustrated in Figure 1-2.

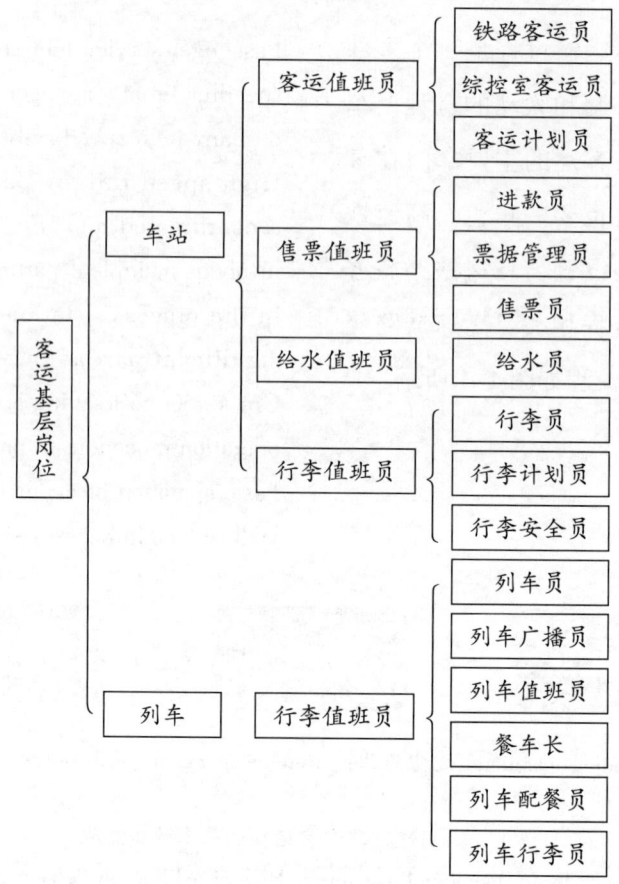

客运基层岗位：passenger service grass-root post　车站：station
客运值班员：passenger service watchman　铁路客运员：railway passenger service worker
综控室客运员：comprehensive office passenger service worker　客运计划员：passenger service planner
售票值班员：ticket selling watchman　进款员：money collector　票据管理员：receipt administrator
售票员：ticket seller　给水值班员：water supply watchman　给水员：water supplier
行李值班员：luggage watchman　行李员：luggage operator　行李计划员：luggage planner
行李安全员：luggage safety operator　列车：train　列车员：luggage operator
列车广播员：train broadcaster　列车值班员：train watchman　餐车长：chief of dinning coach
列车配餐员：train pantry man　列车行李员：train luggage operator

图 1-2　高速铁路客运基层岗位结构
Figure 1-2　High Speed Railway Passenger Service Grass-root Post Structure

高速铁路基层客运岗位的主要操作岗位包括：铁路客运员、综控室客运员、客运计划员、进款员、票据管理员、售票员、给水员、行李员、行李计划员、行李安全员、列车员、列车广播员、列

Major operating posts at the grass-root level include: train passenger service worker, comprehensive office passenger service worker, passenger service planner, money collector, receipt administrator, ticket seller, water supplier, luggage operator,

车值班员、餐车长、列车配餐员、列车行李员等。

铁路基层客运管理岗位包括：客运值班员、售票值班员、给水值班员、行李值班员、列车长。

luggage planner, luggage safety worker, coach worker, train broadcaster, train watchman, chief of dinning coach, pantry man, luggage operator and so on.

Management posts at the grass-root level include: passenger service watchman, ticket selling watchman, water supply watchman, luggage watchman and conductor.

学习笔记
Study Notes

模块三 课堂练习

分小组讨论高速铁路各基层客运工作岗位的工作内容。

Module 3 In-class Exercises

Discuss the main work of the high speed railway passenger service at the grass-root level in groups.

课堂练习
In-class Exercises

模块四 课后拓展

高速铁路客运工作应遵守哪些法律、法规和规章?

Module 4　After-class Activity

Which laws, rules and regulations shall be complied with in high speed railway passenger service?

任务二 高速铁路客运服务概述

Task 2　Overview of High Speed Railway Passenger Service

模块一　学前准备

Module 1　Preparation before Class

昆明刚开通高铁，有一位不识字的老人首次乘坐高铁，想寻求客运服务人员的帮助，作为客运服务人员应该怎么帮助老人？

High speed railway has just been introduced in Kunming, and an illiterate elder took the high speed railway for the first time and wanted the help. How can the service employee help him?

课前学习笔记
Study Notes before Class

模块二　课堂学习

知识点一：高速铁路客运服务的基本原则

1. 旅客至上

随着市场经济的不断深入，铁路运输企业面对的是一个竞争的运输市场，铁路服务必须树立"旅客至上"的理念。高速铁路客运服务人员要变"以我为主"为"以客为主"，真正从内心深处把旅客当成我们的"衣食父母"。

2. 用心服务

铁路运输每天要接待数以万计的旅客，特别是春运、节假日等特殊时期，旅客出行的人数更多，如何在繁杂劳累的工作中保持良好的服务礼仪，必须从内心去感受和体会礼仪服务的重要性和必要性，养成礼仪服务的职业习惯，做到服务发自内心。同时，用心服务还包括通过各种方式获知旅客的需求信号，主动发现服务机会，并提供及时、恰当、满意的服务以满足旅客的高期望值。

3. 持之以恒

服务礼仪作为规范化服务的重要内容之一，不会自发形成，而是需要进行严格的岗位培训。动车组站车服务人员要保持心理平衡，维系一种良好的服务

Module 2　In-class Learning

Key Point 1: Basic Principles of High Speed Railway Passenger Service

1. Passenger First

With the deepening of market economy, railway service shall bear in mind the concept of "passenger first" in the competitive transportation market. The concept of "self oriented" of the service employees' shall be change into "passenger oriented" and the employees shall really treat passengers as the "resource of the revenue".

2. Wholehearted Service

There are tens of thousands of passengers each day in railway transportation, and there are even more during Spring Festival, holidays and other special periods. The key to keep good service etiquette in the complex and arduous work is to feel the importance and necessity of the etiquette to form the professional habit of serving from the heart. Meanwhile, wholehearted service also means recognizing passengers' demand signal, initiative discovering of service opportunity and instant, proper, satisfying service to meet passengers' high expectations.

3. Persistence

Service etiquette, as an important part of standard service, does not arise spontaneously, it requires strict post training. Service employees at the stations and in the trains of the high speed railway should

心态，才能将职业要求逐步变成职业习惯，并持之以恒。只有保持长久的服务礼仪，才能从根本上形成良好的服务规范。

知识点二：高速铁路客运服务心理

1. 客运服务人员服务心理的基本原则

（1）服务的内涵。

很多矛盾冲突往往是由于双方在交际过程中缺乏彼此的尊重所造成的，比如，客运服务人员对于有意见的乘车旅客反唇相讥、拿旅客的言行当谈资、以貌取人等，造成旅客对服务态度的投诉。因此，客运服务人员首先要学会尊重旅客，把握尊重他人、理解他人的服务内涵，学习从旅客的角度看待和处理问题。

（2）热情待客。

客运服务人员在工作中不仅不能怠慢、排斥、挑剔旅客，而且还应积极、热情、主动地接近旅客，淡化彼此之间的戒备、抵触和对立情绪，将旅客当作自己家人看待。

（3）重视旅客。

客运服务人员对旅客的尊重应表现为真诚对待旅客，并且主动关心旅客的需求和感受。

（4）赞美旅客。

客运服务人员应善于发现旅客的优点并进行发自内心的赞美。从心理学的角度来讲，每个人都喜欢听赞美之词，

keep psychological balance and good service psychology to form professional habit gradually and persistently. In this way, good service standard is formed fundamentally.

Key Point 2: Passenger Service Psychology

1. Basic Principle of Service Psychology

（1）Connotation of service.

Most conflicts arise due to the lack of respect during communication, for example, service employees snap the passenger with whom they are not satisfied, or they judge passengers with their appearance, talk about them and so on, and lead to passengers' complaints about the attitude. Therefore, passenger service employees shall learn to respect passengers, grasp the service connotation of respecting and understanding other, and to treat and deal with problems from the passengers' perspective.

（2）Treat passengers warmly.

Instead of slow, repulsive and choosy service, passenger service employees shall serve actively and warmly, and treat passengers as family members to eradicate defensive, contradicting and oppositive emotion.

（3）Attach importance to passenger service.

Passenger service employees shall treat passengers sincerely and pay attention to their need and feelings actively.

（4）Praise passenger.

Passenger service employees shall look for the merits of passengers and praise them

所有人都希望自己能够得到别人的欣赏与肯定。

2. 高速铁路客运服务人员的角色定位

（1）客运服务人员是旅客的秘书，大部分旅客对动车组设备、设施和服务内容都没有客运服务人员清楚，客运服务人员应该向旅客进行耐心解释和热情服务，消除旅客的疑惑，为旅客提供满意的服务。

（2）旅客是铁路及客运服务人员的衣食父母，客运服务人员的工作职责就是为旅客提供满意的服务，让旅客感觉到"宾至如归"，想旅客之所想，急旅客之所急，这样才能提升旅客的满意度和信任度。绝不能对旅客不理不睬，置若罔闻。

（3）客运服务人员还应根据所在行业的服务特点，在服务内涵方面进行准确定位，按照社会对自己所扮演的角色的常规要求、限制和看法，来对自己的形象进行设计。

3. 高速铁路客运服务人员服务意识

（1）服务意识是满足旅客潜在需求的服务能力。客运服务人员要能及时、准确地发现旅客的潜在需求，主动关注旅客，学会察言观色，主动与旅客沟通，通过旅客的言行举止来发掘旅客的潜在需求，尽可能地满足旅客的要求。

from heart. In terms of psychology, people like to hear praise and hope to be appreciated and confirmed.

2. Role Orientation of Passenger Service Employee

（1）Passenger service employee is the secretary of passengers, and most passengers are not familiar with the equipment, devices and service in the high speed trains. Therefore, employees shall explain to passengers patiently and serve them warmly to reassure them and provide them with satisfactory service.

（2）The duty of the passenger service employees is to provide satisfactory service to passengers, who are the "source of revenue" of the railway and employees, to make them "feel at home". Satisfaction and trust of passengers is raise through timely consideration and service for the passengers. Negligence of passengers is forbidden.

（3）Passenger service employees shall orientate service connotation precisely based on the features of the industry, and design images according to the social requirement, limit and opinions about the role.

3. Service Awareness of Passenger Service Employees

（1）Service awareness is the ability to satisfy the potential need of passengers. It is required that employees discover the potential need of passengers, pay attention to them actively, observe carefully and communicate positively, and then to discover their potential need through their words and behaviors,

（2）积极主动地为旅客着想。列车客运服务人员身负为旅客服务的责任，应该积极主动地为旅客考虑，为旅客排忧解难。

（3）耐心周到地为旅客服务。客运服务人员应该根据不同旅客的性格特点，耐心地为旅客办理业务、解答咨询，用心为旅客服务。

4. 高速铁路客运服务人员的服务心态

很多客运服务人员在服务旅客的过程中受到旅客情绪波动的影响或由于工作中不顺心的事情而影响了为旅客服务时的态度和质量，牢骚满腹，甚至将不高兴的情绪传染给所服务的旅客，这必然会对旅客的感受产生影响，导致旅客不满意。我们应清醒地认识到为旅客服务是每一位客运服务人员的基本职责，不应该把自己的情绪带到工作中来，不能影响铁路对外的形象。如果不积极调整自己的情绪，没有大局观念，就会直接影响到旅客的满意度和自己的发展。

5. 高速铁路客运服务人员的服务技能

（1）客运服务人员应该掌握的基本技能包括：服务礼仪、专业知识、业务技能等。

（2）对于一名客运服务人员来说，仅仅具备很好的工作态度和服务意识是不够的。如果不具备工作职责所要求的

satisfy their need as much as possible.

（2）Considerate for passengers actively. Passenger service employees bear the responsibility of passenger service, so they shall considerate for passengers active and help them to solve problems.

（3）Serve passengers patiently and thoughtfully. Service employees shall handle the requirement and answer questions of the passengers patiently according to different characters of the passenger and serve them wholeheartedly.

4. Service Psychology of Passenger Service Employees

Some service employees' attitude and service quality is affected as a result of their mood swings or personal frustration, or they even affect passengers with the negative mood. It will result in passengers' dissatisfaction. It shall be realized clearly that it is the service employees' fundamental duty to serve every passenger, personal mood shall not affect work and the image of the railway. Failure to adjust the mood actively and lack of comprehensive vision will directly affect passengers' satisfaction and personal development.

5. Service Skills of Passenger Service Employees

（1）Basic skills of passenger service employees include: service etiquette, professional knowledge and skills.

（2）Good work attitude and service awareness is not enough for a service employee. Lack of necessary and basic skills will not guarantee good passenger service and errors in

基本技能，就不能很好地为旅客服务，工作中出现的差错同样是造成旅客投诉的重要因素。

6. 高速铁路客运服务人员的自我改进

（1）运输行业在日益激烈的市场竞争环境下，企业之间的产品和服务日趋同质化，服务的创新已成为各企业争取和挽留旅客的有力武器。列车客运服务人员服务素养的改进是铁路维系和拓展市场份额、应对激烈竞争的重要举措，也是服务创新的基础。

（2）自我改进是客运服务人员提高服务质量永恒的主题。不进则退，这是我们众所周知的发展规律，客运服务人员面对旅客的期望和需要要不断地提升服务质量，只有不断总结、取长补短，学习新的服务理念和服务模式，以提升自身的服务技能和服务素养，才是赢得市场认可的有效途径。

work is the important reason of passengers' complaints.

6. Self-improvement of High Speed Railway Service Employee

（1）Products and service of different enterprises are homogeneous in the competitive transportation industry, and service innovation is the efficient method to win and retain more passengers. Service quality improvement is a significant measure to maintain and expand market ratio to face the fierce competition for railways, and it is also the basis for innovation.

（2）Self-improvement is the eternal theme for the improvement of service quality. "No advance means going back", it is a well-known rule. Passenger service employees shall improve service quality to meet passengers' expectation and need. Continuous summary, learning from others for self-improvement to get new service concept and mode, to improve service skill and quality, is the efficient way to win market recognition.

学习笔记
Study Notes

模块三　课堂练习

Module 3　In-class Exercises

某高铁站,其中一台取票设备损坏,乘客在该设备前不知所措,工作人员发现后应当如何处理?

One of the ticket collection equipment is broke down, and a passenger is at loss, how does the service employee deal with the situation?

图 1-3　高铁站取票设备

Figure 1-3　Ticket Collection Equipment at the Hgh Speed Railway Station

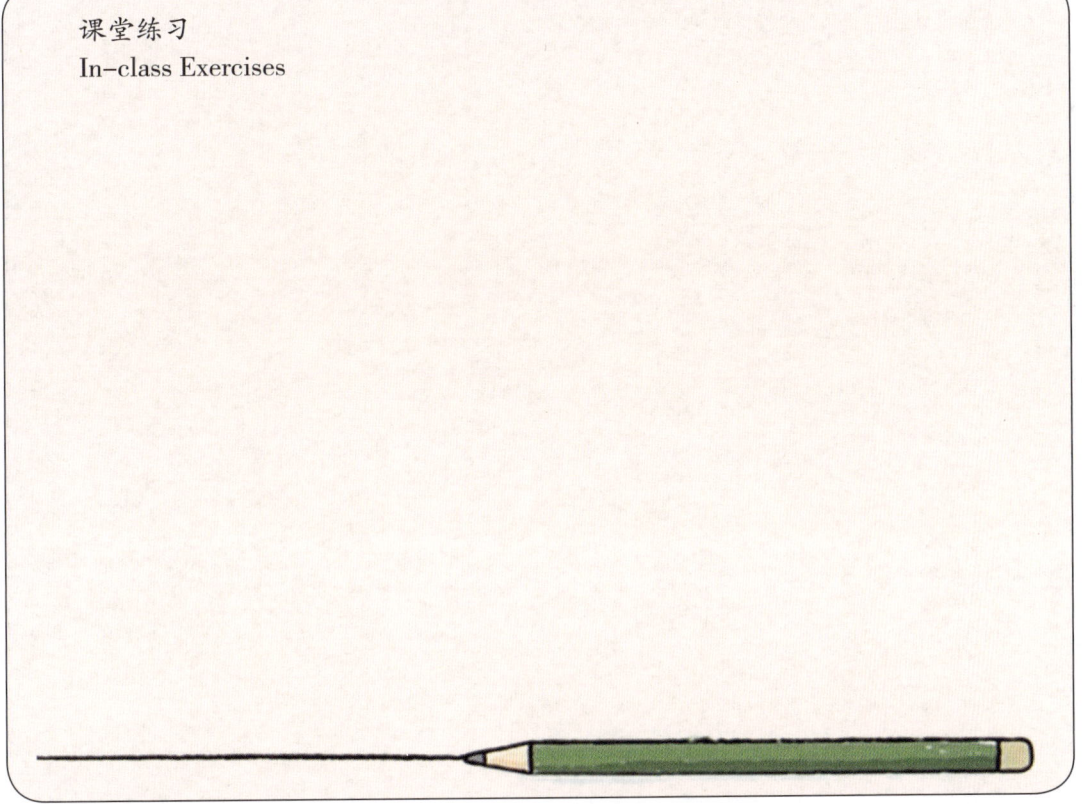

课堂练习
In-class Exercises

模块四　课后拓展

为什么高速铁路客运服务工作中要严格遵守各项工作制度？

Module 4　After-class Activity

Why the working regulations shall be followed strictly in the process of passenger service?

After-class Activity

项目二　高速铁路客运服务礼仪

Project 2　High Speed Railway Passenger Service Etiquette

任务一　礼仪概述

Task 1　Etiquette Overview

模块一　学前准备

Module 1　Preparation before Learning

礼仪的概念和内涵是什么？

What is the concept and connotation of etiquette?

课前学习笔记
Study Notes before Class

模块二　课堂学习

知识点一：礼仪的概念

礼仪是人们在社会交往中受历史传统、风俗习惯、宗教信仰、时代潮流等因素的影响而形成的，既为人们所认同，又为人们所遵守，是以建立和谐关系为目的的各种符合礼的精神及要求的行为准则和规范的总和。

礼仪经过不断发展，成为人类维系社会正常生活而共同遵守的道德规范并以风俗、习惯和传统等方式固定下来。对一个人来说，礼仪是一个人的思想道德水平、文化修养、交际能力的外在表现；对一个社会来说，礼仪是一个国家社会文明程度、道德风尚和生活习惯的反映。礼仪包括"礼"和"仪"两部分。

知识点二：礼仪的内涵

从广义上讲，礼仪是人们在社会交往活动中形成的行为规范与准则，是礼节、礼貌、仪表、仪式等的总称，其涉及社会、道德、习俗、宗教等方面，是个人道德、修养程度及社会整体文明的一种外在表现形式。

从狭义上讲，礼仪指的是国家、政府机构或人民团体、企业机构在正式活动和一定环境中采取的行为、语言等规

Module 2　In-class Learning

Key Point 1：Concept of Etiquette

Etiquette forms in the process of social interaction under the influence of historical tradition, customs and habits, religious believes and trends of the times and so on. It is recognized and observed by people, and the sum of standards and rules in compliance with formal spirits and requirements aiming to building harmonious relationships.

In the process of development, etiquette is fixed to be the moral regulation observe by all people in the forms of customs, habits and traditions. For a single person, etiquette is the external manifestation of his moral standard, cultural attainment and communications skills; for a society, it is the reflection of a nation's civilized degree, morality and habits. Etiquette includes politeness and deportment.

Key Point 2：Connotation of Etiquette

In a broad sense, etiquette is the operative rules and standards formed in social interactions and the sum of deportment, politeness, appearance and ceremony, it involves the aspects of society, morality, customs and religious. It is the external manifestation of personal morality, culture and social civilization.

In a narrow sense, it is the behavioral and lingual standards adopted by a nation, government, civil organization, enterprises in official activities or under certain

范，是在较大或较隆重的正式场合，为表示对接待对象的尊重所举行的合乎社交规范和道德规范的仪式；是社会交往中在礼遇规格、礼宾次序等方面应遵循的礼貌、礼节要求，一般通过集体的规范仪式和程序行为来体现。

知识点三：礼仪的分类

礼仪存在于人们日常生活、工作中的各个方面，礼仪无处不在。根据礼仪的运用环境不同，可将礼仪分为以下几类。

1. 个人礼仪

人是礼仪的行为主体，所以讲礼仪首先应该从个人礼仪开始。个人礼仪包括言谈举止、仪表服饰等多方面的礼仪要求。个人的形体礼仪、仪态礼仪、仪表礼仪、修养等均属于个人礼仪范畴。

2. 生活礼仪

生活礼仪包括生活中的各类情景所须遵循的礼仪。例如：见面交谈礼仪、介绍宴请礼仪、校园礼仪、聚会礼仪、饮食礼仪、送礼礼仪、探病礼仪、结婚礼仪、祝寿礼仪、节庆礼仪、殡葬礼仪等。

3. 社交礼仪

社交礼仪更为繁杂，通常包括见面与介绍礼仪、拜访与接待礼仪、交谈与

circumstances. It is the ceremony in compliance with social and moral regulations to show respect for the guest; it is also the polite and ceremonial requirement in terms of courteous specification and reception order to be reflected through group standard ceremony and procedural behavior.

Key Point 3: Classification of Etiquette

Etiquette exists in every aspect of people's daily life and work. Etiquette can be classified as follows based on the circumstances it is sued.

1. Personal Etiquette

People are the subjects of etiquette, therefore, etiquette starts from personal etiquette. Personal etiquette includes manners and speech, appearance and apparel. Personal body rites, deportment, appearance and cultivation belongs to personal etiquette.

2. Life Etiquette

Life etiquette includes etiquette to be followed in various situations in life, namely, conversation, introduction and treating, campus, party, drinking and eating, gift giving, patient visit, wedding, birthday celebrating, festival, funeral and so on.

3. Social Etiquette

Social etiquette is more complicated, it generally includes meeting and introduction, visit and reception, conversation and

交往礼仪、宴请与馈赠礼仪、舞会与沙龙礼仪等。

4. 服务礼仪

服务礼仪是指各类服务行业的从业人员，在自己的工作岗位上所应遵守的礼仪。如高铁客运服务礼仪、酒店服务礼仪、航空服务礼仪等。

5. 公务礼仪

公务礼仪是具体工作产生的礼仪，如办公室礼仪、交接礼仪、会议礼仪、公文礼仪、公务礼仪、迎送礼仪等。

6. 商务礼仪

商务礼仪是指商务活动中的礼仪，包括柜台待客礼仪、商业洽谈礼仪、推销礼仪、商务文书礼仪、公关礼仪等等。

7. 其他礼仪

其他礼仪如习俗礼仪、民族礼仪、宗教礼仪、涉外礼仪等。

知识点四：高速铁路客运服务礼仪

高速铁路客运服务礼仪是指高速铁路客运服务人员在高速铁路车站、动车组服务工作中向旅客表示敬意的仪式和礼节，是高速铁路客运服务礼仪、礼貌、规范的总称，是高速铁路客运服务人员

communication, entertainment and gift giving, ball and saloon etiquette and so on.

4. Service Etiquette

Service etiquette is to be observed by all employees in service industry. Such as high speed passenger service, hotel hospitality and aviation hospitality and so on.

5. Official Business Etiquette

Official business etiquette is specified in the process of work, such as office, handover, conference, official document, business affairs, greeting and seeing-off and so on.

6. Business Etiquette

It refers to the etiquette in the process of business affairs, such as reception, business negotiation, sales, business document, public relations and so on.

7. Other Etiquette

Other etiquette include customs, ethnic culture, religion, foreign affairs and so on.

Key Point 4: High Speed Railway Passenger Service Etiquette

Passenger service etiquette is the sum of service etiquette, politeness and regulations that the service employees showing respect to passengers in high speed railway stations and CRH service. It is the service standards and post requirement to be followed by the service employees. It is the occupational requirement

必须遵循的服务规范和岗位要求。它不仅是高速铁路客运服务人员的工作需要，也是塑造良好铁路企业形象的需要。

高速铁路客运服务礼仪示例如图 2-1 所示。

for all employees and also the demand to keep the good image of railway enterprises.

The high speed railway passenger service etiquette is illustrated in Figure 2-1.

图 2-1 服务礼仪示列

Figure 2-1　Service Etiquette Illustration

学习笔记
Study Notes

模块三　课堂练习

分小组练习高速铁路客运服务礼仪。

Module 3　In-class Exercises

Discuss high speed railway passenger service etiquette in groups.

课堂练习
In-class Exercises

模块四　课后拓展

礼仪的起源是什么？礼仪是如何发展的？

Module 4　After-class Activity

What is the origin and development of etiquette?

After-class Activity

任务二 高速铁路客运服务仪容仪表礼仪

Task 2 High Speed Railway Passenger Service Appearance Etiquette

模块一 学前准备

Module 1 Preparation before Class

高速铁路客运服务人员仪容仪表要求有哪些?

What are the requirement for the appearance of high speed railway passenger service employees?

课前学习笔记
Study Notes before Class

模块二 课堂学习

一个人的仪容仪表往往与他的生活情调、思想修养、道德品质和文明程度密切相关。高铁客运服务人员必须注意自身的仪容仪表，给旅客留下良好的印象。

知识点一：仪容仪表要求

为了树立良好的服务形象，高铁客运服务人员需要严格要求自己的仪容仪表。一名优秀的服务人员必须着装整洁、大方，面带笑容，主动向客人问候。

1. 发型

（1）整齐利落、清洁清爽。
（2）发长过肩的女性必须将头发束起，佩戴发网，将头发绾于发网内，如图2-2所示。

Module 2　In-class Learning

A person's appearance is often related to his life sentiment, mental cultivation, morality and degree of civilization. Passenger service employees shall pay attention to personal appearance to present good service image to passengers.

Key Point 1：Appearance Requirement

Service employees shall make strict demands for personal appearance to build a good service image. A qualified employee shall dress cleanly and tidily, behave elegantly with smile and greet passengers actively.

1. Hair Style

（1）Orderly and neatly, clean and fresh.
（2）Female employee with hair over shoulder length shall tie up the hair with snood, as illustrated in Figure 2-2.

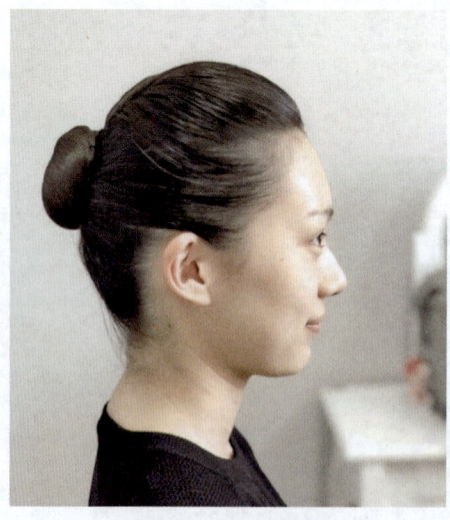

图 2-2　束发示意
Figure 2-2　Hair Coil

（3）男性要剪短发，具体要求为"前发不覆额，侧发不掩耳，后发不及领"，如图2-3所示。

（3）Male employee shall wear short hair, specific requirement is that hair "not attaching to the forehead in the front, not cover the ears on the sides and not touching collar in the back", as illustrated in Figure 2-3.

图 2-3　男性发型示意

Figure 2-3　Male Hairstyle

2. 面容

（1）女性上岗应化淡妆，保持清洁的仪容，避免使用味道浓烈的化妆品，如图2-4所示。

2. Face

（1）Female employees shall wear light make-up, keep tidy appearance and avoid cosmetics with strong smells, as illustrated in Figure 2-4.

图 2-4　女性面容

Figure 2-4　Face（Female）

（2）男性应保持脸面洁净，不可留胡须，如图2-5所示。

（2）Male employee shall keep clean face and wear no moustache, as illustrated in Figure 2-5.

图 2-5　男性面容
Figure 2-5　Face（Male）

（3）适时保持亲切的笑容，如图2-6所示。

（3）Keep warm smile at the proper time, as illustrated in Figure 2-6.

图 2-6　笑容
Figure 2-6　Warm Smile

常见错误：化浓妆或怪异妆；工作时化妆；使用味道浓烈的化妆品；男员工留胡须。

Common mistakes: strong or strange make-up; making-up during work; using cosmetics with strong smell; male employees with moustache.

3. 口腔

（1）保持牙齿、口腔清洁。

（2）定期除掉牙齿上的尼古丁痕迹。

（3）去除吸烟过多而引起的口腔异味。

常见错误：工作前食用葱、蒜、韭菜等带有刺激性气味的食物。

4. 指甲

（1）时刻保持指甲干净整齐，经常修剪。

（2）只可涂肉色和透明色指甲油。

常见错误：指甲过长、使用指甲装饰品。

知识点二：着装要求

高速铁路客运服务人员的服饰应整洁大方，并与高速铁路客运服务的工作性质相协调。

1. 制服

（1）干净无褶皱。

（2）领口、袖口要保持整洁干净，衬衫放在裤子里侧。

（3）裤袋限放工作证等扁平物品或体积微小的操作工具，避免服装变形。

（4）季节更替时，应按规定更换制服，不得擅自替换。

如图2-7所示。

3. Oral Cavity

（1）Keep clean teeth and cavity.

（2）Wipe nicotine traces regularly.

（3）Remove strange smell resulting from smoking.

Common mistakes: eat food with strong smell before work, such as shallot, garlic and leek.

4. Nail

（1）Keep nails tidy and clean, trim them frequently.

（2）Polish nail only with flesh color or transparent nail polish.

Common mistakes: long nails, using nail decorations.

Key Point 2: Dressing Code

Employees' dress shall be tidy and neat to be coordinated with the work features of the urban rail transit.

1. Uniform

（1）Clean with no crease.

（2）Tidy and clean collar and sleeves, shirt tucked in the trousers.

（3）Only flat and small tools such as employee's card can be put in the trousers pocket to avoid deform of dress.

（4）Uniforms shall be changed based on season changes according to regulations, no unauthorized replacement.

As illustrated in Figure 2-7.

图 2-7 制服示意
Figure 2-7 Uniform

常见错误：制服上有异味或污渍；在套装和衬衫的胸袋内放入钱包、硬币等物品；缺扣、立领、挽袖、挽裤。

Common mistake: peculiar smell or stains on uniforms; wallets or coins in the chest pocket of the uniform; lack of button, stand collar, or rolling up sleeves and trousers.

2. 鞋袜

（1）穿着制服时应按规定穿黑色或深色的皮鞋，鞋面保持干净，黑色皮鞋配深色袜子。

（2）女员工着裙装时，长袜应选择与肌肤相贴近的自然色或暗色系中的浅色。

（3）皮鞋应定期清洁，保持干净光亮。

常见错误：穿磨损严重的鞋及露脚趾脚跟的鞋、穿图案过多的袜子。

2. Shoes and Socks

（1）Black or dark color leather shoes shall be worn with uniforms, keep the shoes clean and wear dark color socks.

（2）Female employee shall wear stocking with similar color to skin and light dark color.

（3）Leather shoes shall be cleaned regularly to keep shining.

Common mistake: wear worn-out shoes and shoes exposing toes and heels, wear socks with to many figures.

学习笔记
Study Notes

模块三　课堂练习

1. 仪容仪表的发型、妆容分组练习。

2. 着装分组练习。

Module 3　In-class Exercises

1. Appearance, hairstyle and make-up exercise in groups.

2. Dressing exercise in groups.

课堂练习
In-class Exercises

模块四 课后拓展

（1）高速铁路客运服务人员在修饰与维护本人仪容仪表时，重点应从哪些方面入手？

（2）高速铁路客运服务人员的着装要求有哪些？

Module 4　After-class Activity

（1）What are the key points for high speed railway passenger service employees keeping appearance?

（2）What is the dress code for passenger service employees?

After-class Activity

任务三 高速铁路客运服务仪态礼仪

Task 3 High Speed Railway Passenger Service Manners and Etiquette

模块一 学前准备

Module 1 Preparation before Study

高速铁路客运服务仪态礼仪有哪些？

What are the manners and etiquette in high speed railway passenger service?

课前学习笔记
Study Notes before Class

模块二 课堂学习

在社交场合中,良好的礼仪姿态能够直接体现出服务人员自身的基本素质,对社会交往有着良好的促进作用。通过规范的站姿训练、坐姿训练、走姿训练、蹲姿训练,以及优雅的手势礼仪训练,可以改变诸多不良体态,使身体姿态变得更加优雅得体,充分展示出良好的职业素养,提升服务类行业的品质形象。

知识点一:站姿训练

1. 站姿的基本要求

(1)头部要正,目光平视正前方,下颌微微内收,颈部保持正直,双肩平展,上身向上挺直,腰部直立,呼吸自然。

(2)双臂自然下垂,贴于身体两侧,虎口向前,手指向下,拇指内收。

(3)收腹、提臀、两腿直立、双膝靠拢。

(4)两脚后跟并拢,脚尖分开,呈45°~60°夹角。

(5)脚趾抓地,重心移至双脚掌上,落在两脚之间。

(6)从身体的侧面看,后脑勺、双肩后侧、臀部、小腿肚、脚后跟应该在一条垂直线上。

(7)脚掌与头顶向两极延伸,臀部与腹部向中间夹紧,髋骨向上提,双肩

Module 2　In-class Learning

Good manners and etiquette shows employees' qualities and are beneficiary for good social communication. Standard training of standing, sitting, walking, squatting and graceful hand postures can correct many bad postures and help to build graceful posture and favorable professional quality and enhance enterprise image.

Key Point 1 : Standing Posture Training

1. Basic Requirement for Standing Postures

(1) Upright head with front and horizontal eyesight, lower jaw adducted sightly, upright neck, straight upper body and waist, breathe naturally.

(2) Both arms droop naturally to body sides, with thumb arch to the front, fingers downward and thumb adducted.

(3) Abdomen adducted, hips lifted, straight legs with knees approached and closed.

(4) Heels closed and toes separated with the angle of 45°~60°.

(5) Toes gripping the ground with gravity center in sole between feet.

(6) Back of the head, back of shoulders, hips, calf and heel shall be in the same vertical line.

(7) Sole and head top extend to the both ends, hip and abdomen closed to the

向下沉。

2. 工作中不同的站姿方式

（1）垂臂式站姿。

双臂自然下垂，双手中指自然分别放于裤缝或裙缝处，手指自然放松，双膝并拢，两腿绷直，脚后跟靠紧，两脚尖并拢，如图2-8所示。

center, hip bone lifted and shoulders droops.

2. Standing Posture during Work

（1）Arms plumbing standing posture.

Arms droop naturally, middle fingers beside trousers or skirts seam naturally, fingers relaxed naturally, knees closed, straight legs with toes closed, as illustrated in Figure 2-8.

图 2-8　垂臂式站姿

Figure 2-8　Standing Posture during Work

（2）腹前握指式站姿。

双手置于腹前（肚脐以下约2厘米）重叠摆放，右手置于左手之上，右手轻轻握住左手，两大拇指收回掌心里，其余手指自然并拢、弯曲，双手从正前方看上去呈心形。双脚呈丁字步（以右脚脚跟为中心，向外打开10°~30°，同时左脚脚跟紧贴右脚脚心，并向身体外侧打开15°~30°，使两脚中间保持在60°的夹角），如图2-9所示。

（2）Finger held in front of abdomen gesture.

Hands folded in front of abdomen（2 cm below belly button）, right hand above left hand and holding left hand. Thumbs in the palm, other fingers closed and curved naturally, hands showing heart shape seen from front. Feet showing T step（heel of right foot as center and open outward with the angle of 10°~30°, heel of left foot close tight to the sole of right foot, and open outward with the angle of 15°~30° keep the angle of the feet of 60°）, as illustrated in Figure 2-9.

图 2-9 腹前握指式站姿
Figure 2-9 Finger Held in Front of Abdomen Gesture

知识点二：坐姿训练

文雅的坐姿能体现出端庄、沉着、稳重、冷静。它是一种静态的仪态造型，是常用姿势之一，不同的坐姿能够传达出不同的意义和感情。

1. 坐姿的基本要求

（1）入座时要轻稳。从座位的左边入，左边出。女士着裙装要先轻拢裙摆，而后入座。

（2）入座后上体自然挺直，挺胸，双膝自然并拢（男士可稍分开，不超过肩宽），双腿自然弯曲，双肩平整放松，双臂自然弯曲，双手自然放在双腿上或椅子、沙发扶手上，掌心向下。

Key Point 2：Sitting Posture Training

Graceful sitting posture reflects demure, composure, steadiness and calmness. It is static posture and a common posture; different sitting postures shows different meaning and emotions.

1. Basic Requirement for Sitting Postures

（1）Taking seat lightly and steadily. Taking and leaving seat from left. Female employee wearing skirts shall gather skirt hemline before taking seat.

（2）Keep upper body straight and chest out after taking seat, knees closed naturally (knees can be separated slight, not broader than shoulder width), legs bend naturally, shoulders straight and relaxed, both arms bend

（3）头正，嘴角微闭，下颌微收，双目平视，面容平和自然。

（4）坐在椅子上，应坐满椅子的2/3，脊背轻靠椅背。

（5）离座时，要自然稳当。

2. 女士常用坐姿

（1）标准式。

身体的重心垂直向下，双腿并拢，大腿和小腿成90°角，两脚内侧并在一起，脚尖朝前。双手虎口相交轻握，放在两腿之间。挺直腰部，面带微笑，如图2-10所示。

naturally, both hands put on the legs, or arms of chairs and sofa, palms downward.

(3) Straight head, corners of moth closed tightly, lower jaw abducted with peaceful and natural appearance.

(4) Occupying 2/3 of the chair and back leaning against chair back slightly.

(5) Leaving seat naturally and steadily.

2. Common Female Sitting Postures

(1) Standard type.

Body gravity straight downward, legs closed, 90° angle of thigh and calf, inner sides of the legs closed, forward toes. Thumb arch crossed slightly between legs. Straight waist, smile, as illustrated in Figure 2-10.

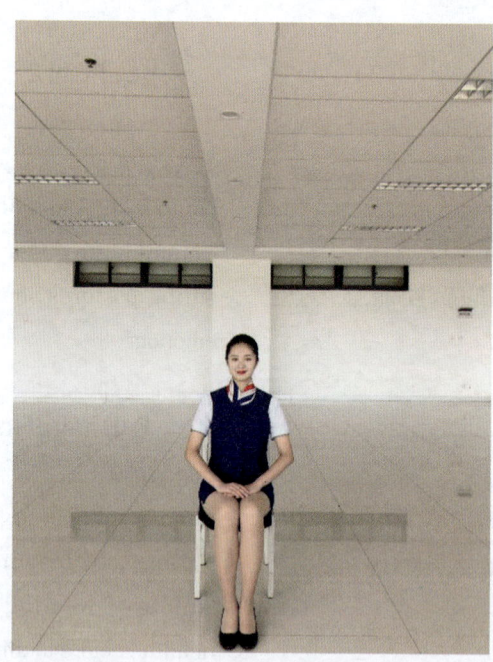

图 2-10 标准式坐姿
Figure 2-10 Standard Type

（2）后屈式。

身体的重心垂直向下，双膝并拢，两小腿向后屈回，脚尖着地。双手虎口相交轻握，放在两腿之间。挺直腰部，面带微笑，如图 2-11 所示。

（2）Bending backward type.

Center of body weight shall be downward with both knees closed together, lower legs bending backward with tiptoes on the ground. Thumb arches crossed between legs. Straight waist with smile, as illustrated in Figure 2-11.

图 2-11　后屈式坐姿

Figure 2-11　Bending Backward Type

（3）伸后屈式。

身体的重心垂直向下，双膝并拢，左脚前伸右脚后屈，或右脚前伸左脚后屈。双手虎口相交轻握，放在两腿之间。挺直腰部，面带微笑，如图 2-12 所示。

（3）Extension and backward bending type.

Body gravity vertically downward, knees closes, left leg extending forward and right leg bending backward or vice versa. Thumb arches crossed between legs. Straight waist with smile, as illustrated in Figure 2-12.

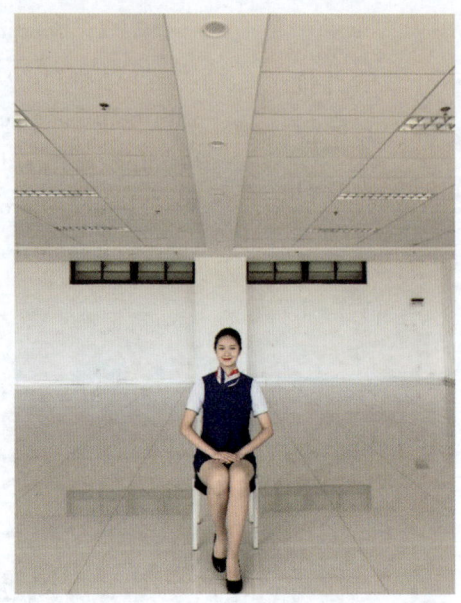

图 2-12　伸后屈式坐姿

Figure 2-12　Extension and Backward Bending Type

（4）前交叉式。

身体的重心垂直向下，双腿大腿并拢，小腿在身体正前方交叉，脚尖向前，双手虎口相交轻握，放在两腿之间，挺直腰部，面带微笑，如图 2-13 所示。

(4) Crossing forward type.

Body gravity downward vertically, thighs closed, calves crossed in front of the body with forwarding toes. Thumb arches crossed between legs. Straight waist with smile, as illustrated in Figure 2-13.

图 2-13　前交叉式坐姿

Figure 2-13　Crossing Forward Type

（5）侧点式。

身体的重心垂直向下，双腿并拢，大腿和小腿成90°角，双脚向左或向右平行移动，使小腿向左或向右倾斜45°，倾斜后两腿保持并在一起，脚尖点地。双手虎口相交轻握，放在两腿之间。挺直腰部，面带微笑，如图2-14所示。

（5）Side point type.

Body gravity downward vertically, legs closed, thigh and calf with the angle of 90°, feet move to the right or the left horizontally, with the angle of the calf of 45° to the left or the right, both legs closed together after inclining tiptoed. Thumb arches crossed between legs. Straight waist with smile, as illustrated in Figure 2–14.

图 2-14 侧点式

Figure 2–14 Side Point Type

图 2-15 侧挂式

Figure 2–15 Side Hanging Type

（6）侧挂式。

在侧点式的基础上，两腿重叠摆放，两脚脚尖绷直，前一只脚的脚尖收回至后一只脚的小腿后方。双手虎口相交轻握，放在处在上方的腿上，挺直腰部，面带微笑，如图2-15所示。

（6）Side hanging type.

On the basis of side point type, legs overlapped with straight toes, toe of the front foot withdrawn behind the calf of the other leg. Thumb arches crossed between legs. Straight waist with smile, as illustrated in Figure 2–15.

3. 男士常用坐姿

（1）标准式。

身体的重心垂直向下，双腿并拢，大腿和小腿成90°，两脚内侧并在一起，脚尖朝前。双手放于大腿靠近膝盖处。挺直腰部，面带微笑。如图2-16所示。

（2）分膝式。

身体的重心垂直向下，两腿平行，两膝分开与肩同宽，小腿与地面垂直，脚尖朝向正前方。双手放于大腿靠近膝盖处。挺直腰部，面带微笑，如图2-17所示。

3. Common Male Sitting Postures

（1）Standard type.

Body gravity vertically downward, legs closed with the thigh and calf angle of 90°, inner sides of the legs closed with forwarding toes. Hands on the thighs near the knees, straight waist with smile. As illustrated in Figure 2-16.

（2）Knee separation type.

Body gravity vertically downward, parallel legs, knees separated with shoulder width, calves perpendicular to the ground with toes straight forward. Hands on the thighs near the knees, straight waist with smile, as illustrated in Figure 2-17.

图 2-16　标准式男坐姿　　　　　图 2-17　分膝式坐姿

Figure 2-16　Standard Type　　　Figure 2-17　Knee Separation Type

知识点三：行姿训练

行姿体现的是高铁客运服务工作人员的基本形象。在工作过程中，行姿代表着企业的形象和精神。

行姿的基本要求

（1）规范的行姿首先要以端正的站姿为基础。

（2）双肩应平稳，以肩关节为轴，双臂前后自然摆动。

（3）上身挺直，头正、挺胸、收腹、立腰，重心稍向前倾。

（4）注意步位。脚尖略开。起步时，身体微向前倾，两脚内侧落地。不要将重心停留在后脚，并注意在前脚着地和后脚离地时要伸直膝部。

（5）步幅适当。一般前脚的脚跟与后脚的脚尖相距为一个脚长左右的距离。步伐稳健，步履自然，要有节奏感，保持一定的速度，如图2-18所示。

Key Point 3: Walking Gesture Training

Walking gesture shows basic image of service employees and it also shows enterprise image and spirit during working.

Basic Requirement for Walking Gesture

(1) Standard walking gesture is based on upright standing posture.

(2) Keep shoulders steady, swing arms forward and backward naturally pivoting shoulder joint.

(3) Keep upper body straight, head upright, head straight, chest out, abdomen abducted, waist upright with body gravity leaning forward slight.

(4) Pay attention to pace position. Toes opens slightly, body leaning forward slightly when start walking, inner sides of feet landing on the ground. Don't leave body gravity on the back foot, and note that keep knees straight when front foot landing on the ground and back foot leaving the ground.

(5) Keep proper pace. Generally speaking, distance between the heel of the front foot and toe of the back foot is the length of one foot, keep steady pace and natural and rythmed walking at a certain speed, as illustrated in Figure 2-18.

图 2-18　行姿
Figure 2-18　Walking Gesture

知识点四：蹲姿训练

蹲姿是人在处于静态时的一种特殊体位，是由站姿转换为两腿弯曲、身体高度下降的姿势，常用于工作人员捡拾物品时。

1. 蹲姿的基本要求

（1）下蹲抬物时，应自然、得体、大方，不遮遮掩掩。

（2）下蹲时，两腿合力支撑身体，避免滑倒。

（3）下蹲时，应使头、胸、膝关节在一个角度上，使蹲姿优美。

（4）女士无论采用哪种蹲姿，都要将腿靠紧，臀部向下。

Key Point 4：Squatting Posture Training

Squatting posture is a static and special body gesture, it transformer from standing posture to leg bending and body descending posture, and is generally adapted in picking up objects on the ground.

1. Basic Requirement for Squatting Posture

(1) Picking up objects in squatting posture shall be done naturally and decently, not secretively.

(2) Both legs supporting the body when squatting to avoid sliding.

(3) Keep head, chest and knee joint in the same angle to present graceful squatting gesture.

(4) Female employees shall keep legs closed tightly and hip downward in any squatting posture.

2.女士常用蹲姿

（1）高低式蹲姿。

下蹲时，双腿不并排在一起，而是左脚在前，右脚稍后。左脚应完全着地，小腿基本上垂直于地面；右脚则应脚掌着地，脚跟提起。此刻右膝低于左膝，右膝内侧可靠于左小腿的内侧，形成左膝高右膝低的姿态。臀部向下，基本上用右腿支撑身体，如图2-19所示。

2. Common Female Squatting Posture

(1) High and low squatting posture.

The two legs are not in the same line when squatting, left foot is in the front and right foot in the back. The left foot is completely on the ground, and the calf is perpendicular to the ground. Right sole is con the ground with heel lifted. In this posture, inner side of the right knee is beside the inner side of the left calf to form the posture of higher left knee and lower right knee. Hip is downward with right leg supporting the body, as illustrated in Figure 2-19.

图 2-19 高低式蹲姿

Figure 2-19 High and Low Squatting Posture

（2）交叉式蹲姿。

交叉式蹲姿通常适用于女性，尤其是穿短裙的人员。它的特点是造型优美典雅。其特征是蹲下后腿交叉在一起。这种蹲姿的要求是：下蹲时，右脚在前，左脚在后，右小腿垂直于地面，全脚着地，右腿在上，左腿在下，两者交叉重

(2) Crossed squatting posture.

Generally speaking, crossed squatting posture is suitable for female employees, especially for those wearing skirt. The posture is elegant and graceful. Legs are crossed after squatting. The requirement of the posture is: right leg in the front and left leg in the back during squatting. Left calf is perpendicular to the ground with the entire foot and the

叠；左膝由后下方伸向右侧，左脚跟抬起，并且脚掌着地；两脚前后靠近，合力支撑身体，上身略向前倾，臀部向下，如图2-20所示。

ground, right leg is crossed above the left leg; left knee extends to the right side from back and downward, left heel is lifted with sole on the ground; the two feet are close from front and back to support the body; the upper body leans forward slightly with hip downward, as illustrated in Figure 2-20.

图2-20　交叉式蹲姿

Figure 2-20　Crossed Squatting Posture

3. 男士常用蹲姿

男士一般选用高低式蹲姿。下蹲时，双腿不并排在一起，而是左脚在前，右脚稍后。左脚应完全着地，小腿基本上垂直于地面；右脚则应脚掌着地，脚跟提起。此刻右膝低于左膝，右膝内侧可靠于左小腿的内侧，形成左膝高右膝低的姿态。臀部向下，基本上用右腿支撑身体，如图2-21所示。

3. Common Male Squatting Posture

Male employees usually squat in high-low posture. The left leg is in the front and right leg in the back, instead of putting the two legs side by side. The left foot is completely on the ground, and the calf is perpendicular to the ground; right sole is on the ground with heel lifted. The right knee is lower than the left knee, and the inner side of the right knee leans against the inner side of the left calf to present the posture of higher left knee and lower right knee with hip downward. The right leg supports the body, as illustrated in Figure 2-21.

图 2-21 男士常用蹲姿
Figure 2-21 Common Male Squatting Posture

知识点五：手势训练

在人与人的沟通中，恰当的手势可以起到强调和辅助的作用，是十分重要的体态语言。手势能表达很多种意思，有时候是一些方向的指示、情谊的传递，有时候能够显露我们真实的心境，甚至也是一种精神上的象征。

1. 手势的基本要求

五指自然并拢，掌心斜向上，上身略微倾向手掌指示的方向，表情自然亲切，目光注视人、物、人的变换过程。

2. 常用的五种手势

（1）横摆式。

五指并拢，手掌伸直掌心倾斜45°，由身体一侧由下而上抬起。肘关节自然弯曲，小臂与手掌呈一条直线，与

Key Point 5：Gesture Training

Proper gesture is used to emphasize and assist in communication and is a significant body language. Gesture expresses many meanings: indication of directions, expression of emotions. It is the real expression of minds and sometimes a spiritual symbol.

1. Basic Requirement for Gesture

Five fingers close naturally with palms upward slant; the upper body inclines slightly to the direction the palm indicating. Eyesight focuses from people to object, and object to people with natural and warm facial expression.

2. Five Common Gestures

（1）Horizontal sway type.

Five finger close together, palm straightens with the center inclines by 45°. Hand raises up from one side of the body, the fore arm and palm is in the same straight line and parallel to the ground. When the hand is 15 cm away from

地面平行，摆到距身体15厘米，并不超过躯干的位置时停止。目视来宾，面带微笑。表示"请进""请这边走"，如图2-22所示。

the body and does not exceed the body, look at the passenger with smile to express "come in please", "this way please", as illustrated in Figure 2-22.

图2-22 横摆式

Figure 2-22 Horizontal Sway Type

图2-23 双臂横摆式

Figure 2-23 Arms Horizontal Sway Type

（2）双臂横摆式。

两臂从身体两侧向前向上抬起，两肘微曲，向两侧摆出，两臂之间保持一定的距离，表示"欢迎大家"，如图2-23所示。

（3）屈臂式。

以右手为例，从身体的右侧前方，由下向上抬起，至上臂离开身体45°时，以肘关节为轴，小臂向左侧摆动，距离身体20°处停住。掌心向上，五指并拢，指尖指向左方，视线随客人由右转向左方，如图2-24所示。

（2）Arms horizontal sway type.

Both arms lift forward and upward from body side, with elbows bending slightly and extending to the two side. Keep certain distance between arms to express "welcome", as illustrated in Figure 2-23.

（3）Arm bending type.

Take the right hand as example, hand lifts upward from the right and front of the body, when the upper arm leaves the body with the angle of 45°, forearm swings to the left side pivoting to the elbow joint, and stops with the angle of 20° off the body. The fives fingers close with palm center upward, finger tips direct to the left and eyesight moves from right to the left with the movement of passengers, as illustrated in Figure 2-24.

图 2-24 屈臂式

Figure 2-24　Arm Bending Type

（4）直臂式。

左手手指并拢，手掌伸直，屈肘从身前抬起，向指引的方向摆去，摆到肩的高度时停止，肘关节基本伸直。表示"请看前方""请您随我来"，如图 2-25 所示。

(4) Straight arm type.

Left hand fingers close with straight palm lifting in front of the body with bent elbow. The hand swings to the indicated direction and stops at the height of the shoulder. Elbow joint straightens to express "please look forward" "please follow me", as illustrated in Figure 2-25.

图 2-25 直臂式

Figure 2-25　Straight Arm Type

（5）斜臂式。

将右手自身前提起后，再向右下摆去，使大小臂成一斜线（可略有弯曲），指尖指向椅子或商品（地面）的具体位置，手指伸直并拢，手、手腕与小臂成一条直线，掌心略微倾斜，手臂与身体呈30°夹角。表示"请坐""请看下方"，如图2-26所示。

（5）Arm slanting type.

Lift the right hand in front of the body and then swing downward to the right, upper arm and forearm forms a slanting line （bending slightly）. finger tip directs to chair or object （on the ground）, fingers straighten and closed to be in the same straight line with hand, wrist and forearm; palm center slants slightly and arm forms an angle of 30° with body to express "please take seat", "please look downward", as illustrated in Figure 2-26.

图 2-26 斜臂式

Figure 2-26　Arm Slanting Type

学习笔记
Study Notes

模块三 课堂练习

分小组练习客运服务礼仪的站姿、坐姿、行姿、蹲姿、手势。

Module 3 In-class Exercises

Practice standing, siting, walking and squatting postures and hand gesture in passenger service etiquette in groups.

模块四 课后拓展

站姿、坐姿、行姿、蹲姿、手势的基本要领是什么？

Module 4　After–class Activity

What are the key points of standing, sitting, walking and squatting postures and hand gesture?

任务四　高速铁路客运服务语言礼仪

Task 4　Language Etiquette of High Speed Railway Passenger Service

模块一　学前准备

Module 1　Preparation before Class

高速铁路客运服务语言礼仪有哪些？

What are the content of high speed railway passenger service language etiquette?

课前学习笔记
Study Notes before Class

模块二 课堂学习

语言是人们交流思想、联络情感的重要工具和手段。俗话说："言为心声，语为人镜。"它是人心灵的体现，是揭示人们心灵的窗户，是为乘客服务的第一工具。

知识点一：问候用语

问候是人际交往中的重要环节。问候是向对方询问安好、致以敬意，或者表示关切之意。问候他人时，具体内容应当既简练又规范。

1. 问候用语的种类

（1）标准式问候用语。

标准式问候用语，即直接问候对方的用语。其常见用法，主要是在问好之前，加上适当的人称代词，或者其他尊称。例如："您好""各位好""女士您好""先生好"等。

（2）时效式问候用语。

时效式问候用语，即在一定的时间范围之内才有作用的问候用语。它的常见用法，是在问好、问安之前加上具体的时间，或者在两者之前加上尊称。例如："早上好""各位下午好""小姐早安""尊敬的旅客晚上好"等。

Module 2 In-class Exercises

Language is an important tool and way to communicate. As the saying goes, "words are the voice of mind, and language is the mirror of people". It is the reflection of minds and also the first language to serve passengers.

Key Point 1: Greeting Language

Greeting is an important part in interpersonal communication to sending regards, respect and care. Content of greeting shall be precise and standard.

1. Types of Greeting language

（1）Standard greeting language.

Standard greeting language is used to greet people directly. The common way is to add proper personal pronouns or title before greeting. For example, "how do you do" "how do you do, madam/sir".

（2）Time-based greeting language.

Time-based greeting language is only used in certain period of time. The common way is to add specific time before greeting or add title between the two parts. For example, "good morning" "good afternoon everyone" "good morning madam" "good evening, dear passengers" and so on.

2. 使用问候用语的注意事项

（1）不论在何种场合，问候时表情应当自然、和蔼、亲切，脸上带着温和的微笑。

（2）客运人员应面带微笑、注视乘客向旅客进行问候。

（3）如果被问候者不止一个人时，可采用以下两种方式进行问候：一是统一对其进行问候，如"大家好""各位午安"。二是采用"由尊而卑"的礼仪惯例，先问候身份高者，然后问候身份低者。

（4）不要出现一言不发、使用"喂""嘿"等不礼貌的语言。

知识点二：迎送用语

迎送用语，主要用于客运人员在工作岗位上欢迎或送别旅客。它可分为两种：

1. 欢迎用语

又叫迎客语。常用的欢迎用语有"欢迎光临""欢迎您的到来""见到您很高兴"等。在使用欢迎用语时，通常应当一并使用问候语，并且必要时还需同时向对方主动施以见面礼，如点头、微笑、鞠躬、握手等。

2. 送别用语

又叫告别用语。常用的送别用语有"再见""慢走""走好""欢迎再

2. Notes of Greeting Language

（1）Keep natural, amiable and warm facial expression with smile when greeting.

（2）Service employee shall keep smiling and look at the passengers.

（3）Two ways can be used when greeting more than one person: the first is to greet all people together, such as "hello everyone" "good noon everyone". The second is to greet in the order of superior to inferior ranks.

（4）Don't keep silent or just saying "hi", or "hello".

Key Point 2: Greeting and Seeing-off Language

Greeting and seeing-off language is used in greeting or seeing passengers off. It can be classified into two types.

1. Greeting Language

It is also called passenger greeting language. Most frequently used sentences are "welcome" "welcome your arrival" "nice to meet you" and so on. Greeting language is used with salutations and saluting with nodding, smile, bowing, handshake and so on, if necessary.

2. Seeing-off Language

It is also called farewell language. Most frequently used languages are "goodbye" "take care" "welcome back again" "have a safe trip" and so on.

来""一路平安"等。

知识点三：应答用语

应答用语，是指客运人员在工作岗位上为旅客服务时，用来回应旅客的招呼或者在答复其询问时，所使用的专门用语。

在客运服务工作中，客运人员所使用的应答用语是否规范，往往直接反映他们的服务态度、服务技巧和服务质量。客运人员在使用应答用语时，要做到：有问必答、灵活多变、热情周到、尽力相助、不失恭敬。

（1）当乘客询问时，应双眼注视乘客，面带微笑说："您好，请讲！"

（2）向乘客致歉时应说："实在对不起！这是我工作上的失误！""给您添了许多麻烦，实在抱歉，请多多原谅！"

（3）受到乘客表扬时说："这是我们应该做的，请多提宝贵意见。"

（4）当你未听清楚乘客的问话时说："很对不起，我没听清楚，请重复一遍好吗？"

知识点四：感谢用语

在人际交往中，使用感谢用语，意在表达自己的感激之意。运用感谢用语，可以使自己的心意被他人所接受，同时也可以展示本人的修养，因为"礼多人不怪"。

Key Point 3: Reply Language

Reply language is used by passenger service employees answering passengers' greeting or questions.

Standard reply language shows employees' attitude, skill and quality of service. Requirements for reply language are: answering all questions, flexible, warm and considerate, try to help, respect.

(1) Look at the passengers' when they are asking with smile, saying "hello, please go ahead".

(2) Apologies: "Sorry, this is my fault." "I apologize for the trouble, please forgive my error."

(3) Answering praise: "This is our duty, I appreciate your valuable advice."

(4) When you did not hear the question: "Sorry, I beg your pardon."

Key Point 4: Gratitude Language

Gratitude language is used for expressing thanks. Using gratitude language helps to make the thanks accepted and show self-cultivation. As the saying goes, "courtesy costs nothing".

1. 使用感谢用语的五种时机

（1）获得他人的帮助时。

（2）赢得他人的理解时。

（3）感到他人的善意时。

（4）婉言谢绝时。

（5）受到他人的赞美时。

2. 感谢用语的三种形式

（1）标准式感谢用语。

通常只包括一个词语——"谢谢"。有些情况下，在使用标准式感谢用语向人道谢时，还可在其前后加上尊称或人称代词，如："张先生，谢谢""谢谢李科长"等，这样做可使其对象性更明确。

（2）加强式感谢用语。

有时，为了强化感谢之意，可在标准式致谢用语之前，加上某些副词。这就是加强式的致谢用语。若对其运用得当，往往会令人感动。最常用的加强式感谢用语有"十分感谢""万分感谢""非常感谢""多多感谢""多谢"等。

（3）具体式感谢用语。

具体式感谢用语，一般是用在因为某一具体事宜而向人致谢。在致谢时，致谢的原因通常一并提及。例如："有劳您了""让您替我们费心了""给您添了不少麻烦""这件事情太让您为我费心了"等。

1. Five Situations Using Gratitude Language

（1）Getting help.

（2）Getting understood.

（3）Feeling good will.

（4）Refuse politely.

（5）Praised.

2. Three Types of Gratitude Language

（1）Standard type.

Usually only one phrase is used "thank you". under some circumstances, title or personal pronoun is added to be more specific, for example, "thank you, Mr Zhang" "thank you, section chief Li".

（2）Emphasized gratitude language.

Some adverbials are added in front of the standard gratitude language. The emphasized gratitude language, if used properly, is moving. The most frequently used gratitude languages are "thank you very much" "thanks a lot" "I appreciate it very much".

（3）Specified gratitude language.

It is used to express gratitude for specific event and the reason for it is usually mentioned. For example, "thank you for help" "thank you for going to so much trouble to..." and so on.

知识点五：道歉用语

在工作中，因种种原因而带给他人不便，或妨碍、打扰对方时，客运人员必须及时地向对方表达自己的歉意。对于道歉用语的使用，不要羞于启齿，不论在谁面前，该道歉时就道歉。一句道歉用语就会化解可能出现的冲突。最常用的道歉用语主要有："抱歉""对不起""请原谅""失礼了""不好意思了""很是惭愧""真过意不去"等。

Key Point 5：Apology Language

Passenger service employees shall apologize in case of causing inconvenience, interrupting or disturbing others. Don't feel embarrassed to apologize. Apologize when it is necessary no matter to whom you should apologize. Proper apology may resolve conflicts. Common apology language are "I apologize" " I'm sorry" "please forgive me（my...）" "please forgive my rudeness" "excuse me" "It's ashamed" "I feel sorry" and so on.

学习笔记
Study Notes

模块三 课堂练习

分组练习问候、迎送、问答、感谢、道歉用语。

Module 3 In-class Exercises

Practice greeting, greeting and seeing-off, reply, gratitude and apology language in groups.

课堂练习
In-class Exercises

模块四　课后拓展

高速铁路客运人员应从哪几个方面注意使用标准的服务语言。

Module 4　After-class Activity

How do high speed railway passenger service employees pay attention to standard service language?

After-class Activity

任务五　高速铁路客运涉外礼仪

Task 5　High Speed Railway Passenger Service Foreign-related Etiquette

模块一　学前准备

Module 1　Preparation before Class

高速铁路客运涉外礼仪有哪些？基本原则和基本要求是什么？

What are the foreign-related etiquette in high speed railway passenger service? What are the basic principles and requirements?

课前学习笔记
Study Notes before Class

模块二　课堂学习

涉外礼仪是指在对外交往或涉外工作中，用以维护自身形象、企业形象和本国形象，并向外宾表示尊重、友好、礼貌的各种礼节、仪式及其惯用形式。它是在长期的国际交往中逐步形成的，是国际通用的礼仪规范。

知识点一：涉外礼仪的原则

涉外礼仪的原则，是根据礼仪通则与涉外交往活动实践，从整体性、普遍性角度加以概括形成的，对涉外交际具有普遍指导意义的一些原则。在对外交往中，必须认真贯彻以下原则。

1. 不卑不亢，注重国格

在涉外活动中，每名相关人员不仅要特别注重国格、人格，维护国家利益、民族尊严以及自己所在单位或企业的权益，而且要注意热情有度，内外有别，保守国家和企业商业秘密。

2. 平等相待，礼尚往来

在涉外交往过程中，我们应该特别注意对任何交往对象都要一视同仁，给予平等的尊重与友好，不要对大国小国、强国弱国、富国穷国亲疏有别，区别对待。在对外交往过程中，言行一定要谨慎，表态要慎重。

Module 2　In-class Learning

Foreign-related etiquette is the ritual, ceremony and forms used to show respect, friendliness and politeness to foreign guests to express self, enterprise and national images.

Key Point 1: Principles of Foreign-Related Etiquette

The principles are formed through foreign affairs based on general etiquette rules in terms of integrity and universality and are the guidance in foreign affairs. The following principles shall be implemented.

1. Neither Overbearing nor Servile, Emphasizing National Dignity

In foreign-related affairs, every employee shall concern national and personal dignity and safeguard national interests, national dignity, and institutional/enterprise interests. Keep national and commercial secrets with warm and proper attitude.

2. Equal Communication and Reciprocal Courtesy

During international communication, everyone shall treat other with equal respect and friendliness, despite the size, power or affluence of the country. Language and behavior shall be cautious make declaration with discretion.

知识点二：涉外礼仪基本要求

当今世界，尽管各国社会形态各不相同，经济发展水平各不相等，民族、人口有多寡之别，国家有大小之分，但是有一点是共同的，即文明民族和国家都很注重礼貌礼节。

1. 注重形象，仪表得体

在国际交往中，人们普遍对交往对象的个人形象倍加关注，不仅因为个人形象真实体现着个人的教养和品位、精神风貌和生活态度，还因为个人的形象总是与国家形象、民族形象、企业形象密切相关。通过个人形象可以如实地体现出对交往对象的重视程度。

2. 以礼待人，称呼得当

称呼，指的是人们在交谈时用以表示彼此关系的名称。在对外交往过程中，人们碰到的头一个问题就是怎样称呼对方才合乎礼仪。在对外交往中，应该严格遵循国际上通行的称呼习惯，丝毫不能大意。在国外，男子通称为"先生"，未婚女子被称为"小姐"，已婚女子被称为"夫人"。

与外国人交往应酬时，尤其是在比较正式的场合，应当选用的称呼主要有以下几种。

Key Point 2: Basic Requirement for Foreign Etiquette

Civilized nations emphasize etiquette despite the state of society, level of economic development, number of the people, size of the nation.

1. Emphasize Image, Proper Appearance

People often pay attention to personal images in international communication, as the image does not only reflect personal cultivation, taste, mental outlook and attitude of life, it also closely related to national, ethnic and enterprise image and reflects the degree of emphasis of the people involved.

2. Treat People with Courtesy and Proper Salutation

Salutation is used to show the relationship of people in communication. In foreign affairs, it is also the first issued to be concerned with. Commonly used international salutation shall be used. Men are called by "sir", unmarried ladies are called by "Ms" and married women by "madam".

The following titles are used in formal occasions when communicating with foreigners.

（1）尊称。

它几乎适用于任何场合，主要包括"先生""小姐""女士"。应当强调的是，在称呼一位妇女时，最好根据其婚否，分别以"小姐"或"夫人"相称。

（2）荣誉性称呼。

在人际交往中，若交往对象拥有在社会上备受重视的学位、学术性头衔、专业技术性头衔、军衔、爵位，例如，"博士""教授""医生""律师""法官""工程师""将军""公爵"等等，均可用作称呼。

（3）公务性称呼。

在公务活动中，一般可以直接以对方的职务相称。例如，可称其为"部长""经理""总裁""科长""主任"等等。不过有的国家并不习惯采用此类称呼。

（4）一般性称呼。

它适用于普通场合，即直接称呼他人的姓氏或姓名。例如，"迈克""史密斯""塞缪尔·亨廷顿""亨利·米勒"等等。

（5）特殊性称呼。

它主要是指对于王室成员或神职人员的专门称呼。例如，"教皇""大主教""陛下""殿下""神父""牧师""拉比"等等。

(1) Respectful titles.

It can be used in almost every occasion, mostly "sir" "Ms" "madam". A lady shall be called by "Ms" or "madam" based on her marital status.

(2) Honourable title.

If people involved bear valued, academic, professional, military or noble titles, the titles such as "PHD" "professor" "doctor" "lawyer" "judge" "engineer" "general" "duke" can be used.

(3) Official title.

Official titles, such as "minister" "manager" "CEO" "section chief" "director" can be used. But the titles may not be proper in some countries.

(4) Ordinary title.

It can be used in ordinary occasions. People can be called by their given names or family names, such as "Mike" "Smith" "Samuel Huntington" "Henry Miller" and so on.

(5) Special title.

It is the specific title for royal families or clergies. Such as "Pope" "Bishop" "Your Majesty" "Your Highness" "Priest" "Pastor" "Rabbi" and so on.

3. 知书达理，遵纪守法

（1）尊重妇女，礼让有节。

尊重妇女是国际社会公认的一条重要的礼仪原则，也是衡量男士是否具有文明教养与礼仪风度的重要标准。在西方社会，日常生活中讲究"女士优先"，是一位男士风度高雅的前提。

（2）入乡随俗，谨言慎行。

对外交往中，人们总认为语言不通是交往时的唯一障碍，其实在某些时候，不了解交往对象所在国的风俗习惯才是最大的障碍。若预先了解了对方的习俗禁忌，你就可以尽量避免犯忌，从而成为一个彬彬有礼、受人欢迎的客人或是一个知书达理、体贴周到的主人。

（3）爱护环境。

爱惜和保护环境，从本质上讲，是对整个人类的爱惜和保护。注重环保作为涉外礼仪的主原则之一，是国际舞台上备受关注的焦点话题。在日常生活里，能否以实际行动"爱护环境"，已被视为一个人有没有教养、讲不讲社会公德的重要标志之一。

知识点三：部分国家礼仪介绍

1. 英国礼仪

英国人在待人接物方面所表现出来的独特风格，往往会给人以深刻的印象。英国人给人的印象是：重视传统、保守

3. Educated and Law-abiding

（1）Respect for Women.

Respect for women is an important principle all over the world and also the standard to judge people's cultivation and etiquette. In western society, Lady first is the necessity for people's grace and elegance.

（2）Observe customs, speak and act with caution.

It is generally believed that language is the only barrier. As a matter of fact, the greatest barrier is the lack of understanding of the social customs and habits. Ere-knowledge of foreign customs and taboos can make a polite and popular guest, or educated and considerate host.

（3）Care for the environment.

Care for and protection of environment is also the care and protection of the mankind. Emphasis on environment protection is among the main principles of foreign-related etiquette and also the focused topic in international occasions. In daily life, actual environment protection action is also one of the significant signs of cultivation and morality.

Key Point 3: Introduction to Etiquette in Some Nations

1. British Etiquette

British style is often impressive. The British images are emphasis on tradition, conservancy and reason, seriousness in

理智、不苟言笑。一般认为，具有绅士风度美誉的英国交际礼仪，是西方社交礼仪的代表。

（1）社交礼仪。

英国人不喜欢被人统称为"English"（英国人或英格兰人），将他们称为"British"（英国人或不列颠人）会使所有的英国人感到满意。

在进行介绍时，一般先少后长，先低后高，先次后要，先客后主，即先介绍年少者、职位低者、次要人员和客人，然后再介绍年长者、职位高者、重要人员和主人。

（2）餐饮礼仪。

英国的宴请方式多种多样，主要有茶会和宴会。茶会包括正式和非正式茶会。英国人在席间不布菜也不劝酒，全凭客人的兴趣取用。一般要将取用的菜吃光才礼貌，不喝酒的人在侍者斟酒时，将手往杯口一放就行。

（3）主要禁忌。

英国人认为 13 和星期五是不吉利的，尤其忌讳 13 日与星期五相遇，这个时候，许多人宁愿待在家里不出门。在英国，忌讳谈论男人的工资、女人的年龄、政治倾向等。

2. 法国礼仪

（1）社交礼仪。

法国是个浪漫的国度，法国人在社

speech and manner. It is generally believed that gentle British manners are the representation of Western manners.

(1) Social etiquette.

The British don't like to be called as English people. British is a satisfactory address to all.

During introducing, the order is from the young to the old, the people with lower rank to the people with higher rank, less important people to more important people, and guest to the host.

(2) Dinning etiquette.

There are many types of dinners banquets, and the main types are tea party and dinners. There are formal and informal tea parties. Guests help themselves during banquets. It is polite to eat up the taken dishes. Those who don't drink cover the cup when waiters serve alcohol.

(3) Main taboos.

British think 13 and Friday are ominous, especially when they are the same day, and most people stay home on that day. And people avoid talking about people's salary, women's age and political stance.

2. French Etiquette

(1) Social etiquette.

France is a romantic nation, and there

交礼仪上非常讲究，主要有以下特点：

①爱好社交，善于交际。

对于法国人来说，社交是人生的重要内容，没有社交活动的生活是难以想象的。

②诙谐幽默，生性浪漫。

法国人在人际交往中大都爽朗热情，善于雄辩，高谈阔论，好开玩笑，讨厌不爱讲话的人，对愁眉苦脸者难以接受。

③渴求自由，纪律不严。

在世界各国中，法国人是最著名的"自由主义者"。一般纪律不严，不大喜欢集体行动。

④自尊心强，偏爱"国货"。

法国的时装、美食和艺术有口皆碑，在此影响之下，法国人拥有极强的民族自尊心和民族自豪感，在他们看来，世间的一切都是法国最棒。

⑤骑士风度，尊重妇女。

法国人崇尚骑士风度，就像英国人崇尚绅士风度一样，即勇敢、智慧、尊重妇女。

（2）餐饮礼仪。

作为举世皆知的世界三大烹饪王国之一，法国人十分讲究饮食。法国人爱吃面食，面包的种类很多；他们大都爱吃奶酪；在肉食方面，他们爱吃牛肉、猪肉、鸡肉、鱼子酱、鹅肝，不吃肥肉、宠物、肝脏之外的动物内脏、无鳞鱼和带刺骨的鱼。

are rich content in French social etiquette, the main features are as follows:

① Fondness and skill of communication.

Communication is important in daily life of French, it is impossible to imagine life without communication.

② Humorous and romantic.

Most French people are enthusiastic, eloquent, talkative and humorous, they don't like the speechless and frowned people.

③ Eager for freedom, lack of discipline.

French people are famous as liberals. They are less disciplined and don't like group activity.

④ Strong self dignity, preference for french goods.

French clothes, gourmet and art win universal praise and the French people have strong ethnic self dignity and pride and regard French goods are the best.

⑤ Chevalier manner and respect for women.

French people advocate chevalier manner, namely bravery, wisdom, and respect for women.

（2）Dinner and banquet etiquette.

As one of the three famous kingdom of cuisine, French people pay much attention to food. They love food made of flour, and there are many types of bread; most of them love cheese; they love beef, pork, chicken, caviar, goose liver; they don't eat fat, pets, other animal internal organs except liver, alepidote fish and fish with bones.

法国人特别善饮，他们几乎餐餐必喝，而且讲究在餐桌上要以不同品种的酒水搭配不同的菜肴。法国人用餐时，允许两手放在餐桌上，但却不许将两肘支在桌子上。在放下刀叉时，他们习惯于将其一半放在碟子上，一半放在餐桌上。

（3）主要禁忌。

法国的国花是鸢尾花。法国人大多喜爱蓝色、白色与红色，他们所忌讳的色彩主要是黄色与墨绿色。法国的国鸟是公鸡，他们认为它是勇敢、顽强的直接化身。与英国人和德国人一样，法国人忌讳"13"与"星期五"。在人际交往之中，法国人对礼物十分看重，但又有其特别的讲究。

3. 德国礼仪

德国人的特点是纪律严明，法制观念极强；讲究信誉，重视时间观念；极端自尊，非常尊重传统；待人热情，十分注重感情。

（1）社交礼仪。

德国人在人际交往中非常重视礼节。与德国人握手时，有必要特别注意以下两点：一是握手时务必要坦然地注视对方；二是握手的时间宜稍长一些，晃动的次数宜稍多一些，握手时所用的力量宜稍大一些。重视称呼是德国人在人际交往中的一个鲜明特点。

French are good at drinking and they almost drink at every dinner. They match different drinks with different dishes. They put both hands (not elbows) on the table when dinning. When putting down knife and fork, they put one half on the plate and the other half on the table.

(3) Main taboo.

National flower of France is irises. Most of them love blue, white and red, and the yellow and dark green is taboo. The national bird is rooster, which is the embodiment of bravery and tenacity. Like British and German, 13 and Friday is taboo. They pay much attention to gifts in social communication.

3. German Etiquette

German characteristic is strict discipline, strong legal concept, value of credit, strong sense of time; extreme self dignity; respect for tradition; warmth and emphasis on emotion.

(1) Social etiquette.

German put much emphasis on etiquette. There are two things to be noted when shaking hands with German: the first is to look at them calmly; the second is to keep handshaking with power for relatively long. Emphasis on title is another feature.

（2）餐饮礼仪。

宴席上，男子坐在妇女和地位高的人左侧，女士离开和返回饭桌时，男子要站起来以示礼貌。请德国人进餐，事先必须安排好。就餐谈话时，不隔着餐桌与坐得较远的人交谈，怕影响别人的情绪。

在肉类方面，德国人最爱吃猪肉，其次才轮到牛肉。以猪肉制成的各种香肠，令德国人百吃不厌。在饮料方面，德国人最欣赏的是啤酒。

（3）主要禁忌。

在所有花卉之中，德国人对矢车菊最为推崇，并且选定其为国花。在德国，不宜随意以玫瑰或蔷薇送人，前者表示求爱，后者则专用于悼亡。德国人对黑色、灰色比较喜欢。对于"13"与"星期五"，德国人极度厌恶。

4. 日本礼仪

日本是一个非常重视社交礼仪的国家，讲究礼节是日本人的生活习俗。

（1）社交礼仪。

初次见面时，日本人对互换名片极为重视。初次见面不带名片，不仅失礼而且对方会认为你不好交往。互赠名片时，要先行鞠躬礼，并双手递接名片。接到对方名片后，要认真看阅，看清对方的身份、职务、公司，用点头动作表示已看清楚对方的身份。

(2) Dinning etiquette.

Men sitting on the left of people with higher rank or women. Men stand up for politeness when women leave and return to the table. Advanced arrangement for dinner is required. Don't talk to people at distance at the table to avoid affecting others.

German prefer pork to beef. They love sausage made of pork and love to drink beer.

(3) Main taboos.

Of all kinds of flowers, they lover cornflowers most and regard it as national flower. They don't send others roses or wild roses, as the former means love and the latter means mourning for the dead. They prefer black and gray. They dislike 13 and Friday.

4. Japanese Etiquette

Japan is a nation of social etiquette and it has become part of their daily life.

(1) Social etiquette.

Japanese emphasize name card exchange on first meeting. Failure to bring name card on first meeting is regarded as impoliteness and unfriendliness. Bowing and name cards exchanging with both hands is required. It is also required to read name card carefully to recognize the title, position, company and other information and nod to show that the information is read carefully.

（2）餐饮礼仪。

日本以优良的餐桌礼仪见称。餐厅若需要脱鞋应注意将鞋尖朝外摆放，通常由同去的女士负责整理。榻榻米的正确坐法是"正座"，即把双膝并拢跪地，臀部压在脚跟上。

（3）主要禁忌。

日本人一般不吃肥肉和猪内脏，有的人不吃羊肉和鸭子。日本人不喜欢紫色，认为是悲伤的色调；最忌讳绿色，认为是不祥之色。他们忌9、4等数字；受西方影响，不少人不喜欢13，更忌讳星期五是13日；他们还忌讳三人一起合影，认为中间的人被左右两人夹着，是不幸的预兆。

5. 韩国礼仪

（1）社交礼仪。

韩国素有"礼仪之国"的称号，韩国人十分重视礼仪道德的培养，尊敬长辈是韩国民族恪守的传统礼仪。在韩国，长者得到特别尊重，在长者面前不能抽烟，与长者谈话要摘掉墨镜。韩国人热情好客，每逢宾客来访，总是根据客人的身份举行适当规格的欢迎仪式。

（2）饮食礼仪。

韩国人平时使用的一律是不锈钢制的平尖儿的筷子。勺子在韩国人的饮食生活中比筷子更重要，它负责盛汤、捞汤里的菜、装饭，不用时要架在饭碗或

（2）Dining etiquette.

Japanese is renowned for dining etiquette. Toe cap is put outward in restaurants where shoes shall be taken off and fellow ladies are responsible to arrange. Proper sitting posture on tatami mats is straight sitting, namely, kneeling with legs closed and hips on the heels.

（3）Major taboos.

Generally speaking, Japanese don't eat fat and haslet, some don't eat mutton and duck. They dislike purple as it is color of sadness, and they avoid green as it is color of bad omen. They don't like number 9 or 4; some are influenced by the westerners and avoid 13, especially date 13 on Friday. They avoid taking picture of three persons, as they think that the man in the middle is crowded by the people on both sides and it is the sign of bad omen.

5. Korean Etiquette

（1）Social etiquette.

South Korea is called nation of etiquette and Koreans emphasize morality cultivation. Respect for the elder is the tradition to be followed strictly. In Korea, the elder are respected, smoking is forbidden with presence of the elder, sunglasses shall be taken off when talking to the elder. Koreans are hospitable and they hold proper ceremonies based on guests' identities.

（2）Dining etiquette.

Koreans use flat-tip chopstick made of stainless steel and spoon is more important than chopsticks in dining. Spoon is used to hold soup, take vegetables from soup, hold rice and is put on bowls or other tableware,

其他食器上，而筷子只负责夹菜。

（3）主要禁忌。

韩国人普遍忌数字"4"，因韩国语中"4"与"死"同字同音，传统上认为是不吉利的。因此，在韩国没有4号楼、4层楼、4号房，军队里没有第4师，宴会厅里没有4号桌，敬酒不能敬4杯，点烟不能连点4人。

总之，每一个国家都有自己独特的礼仪，因此，我们在对外交往和服务工作中，要了解一些外国的礼仪习俗，特别要注意其礼仪中的禁忌，以免在工作中引起误解和矛盾。

chopsticks are only used to pick dishes.

（3）Major taboos.

Most Koreans avoid number 4, as its pronunciation is similar with word "death", and is traditionally regarded as bad omen. Therefore, there is no building number 4, 4th floor, room number 4, division 4 in the army, table number 4 in restaurants. And it is also avoided to propose toasts 4 times and ignite cigarettes for 4 persons successively.

In a word, etiquette is every nation is unique. In foreign affairs and service, it is necessary to understand foreign etiquette, especially the taboos to avoid misunderstanding and contradictions.

学习笔记
Study Notes

模块三 课堂练习

分组模拟练习：当你遇到英国人、法国人、德国人、日本人、韩国人时，你该如何进行自我介绍。

Module 3　In-class Exercises

Simulation exercise in groups: how do you introduce yourself when meeting British, French, German, Japanese and Korean.

课堂练习
In-class Exercises

模块四 课后拓展

除本书介绍的五个国家的礼仪外，了解东南亚国家的礼仪。

Module 4　After-class Activity

Try to understand etiquette in South-east Asian countries apart from the etiquette of the above-mentioned five countries.

After-class Activity

项目三 售票作业

Project 3　Ticket Selling

任务一　车票认知

Task 1　Recognize Train Ticket

模块一　学前准备

通过互联网搜索至少五个国家正在使用的火车票样式，并进行对比分析。

Module 1　Preparation before Learning

Search train tickets in use in five different countries at least on Internet, analyze and compare them.

课前学习笔记
Study Notes before Class

模块二 课堂学习

知识点一：车票的作用及分类

1. 作用

车票的作用体现在以下几个方面：

（1）铁路旅客运输合同的组成部分。

（2）铁路旅客运输合同的书面形式。

（3）铁路旅客运输合同的凭证。

（4）旅客运输的凭证。

（5）资格凭证。

（6）纸质车票是报销凭证。

2. 分类

车票是乘车票据的总称。

Module 2　In-class Learning

Key Point 1: Function and Classification of Train Ticket

1. Function

Functions of train tickets are as follows：

（1）Components of railway passenger transit contract.

（2）The written form of railway passenger transit contract.

（3）Certificate of railway passenger transit contract.

（4）Certificate of passenger transit;

（5）Qualification certificate.

（6）Paper ticket is certificate for reimbursement.

2. Classification

Ticket is the summary of training taking ticket.

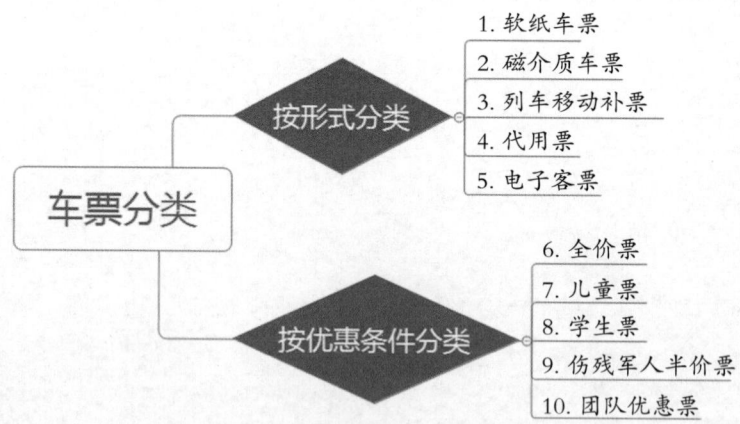

车票分类：classification of train ticket　　按形式分类：classification by form　　软纸车票：soft ticket
磁介质车票：magnetic medium ticket　　列车移动补票：mobile ticket　　代用票：substituting ticket
电子客票：electronic ticket　　按优惠条件分类：classification by favorable conditions
全价票：full price ticket　　儿童票：child ticket　　学生票：student ticket
伤残军人半价票：half rate ticket for wounded and disabled servicemen　　团队优惠票：discount ticket for groups

图 3-1　车票的分类

Figure 3-1　Classification of Train Ticket

（1）软纸车票。

软纸车票如图 3-2 所示。普速列车车票与动车组列车车票均可用软纸车票打印。白背红底，供普通制票机使用。

(1) Soft ticket.

As illustrated in Figure 3-2, ticket for ordinary and high speed railway trains can be printed on soft train ticket with white back and red background and used in ordinary ticket printers.

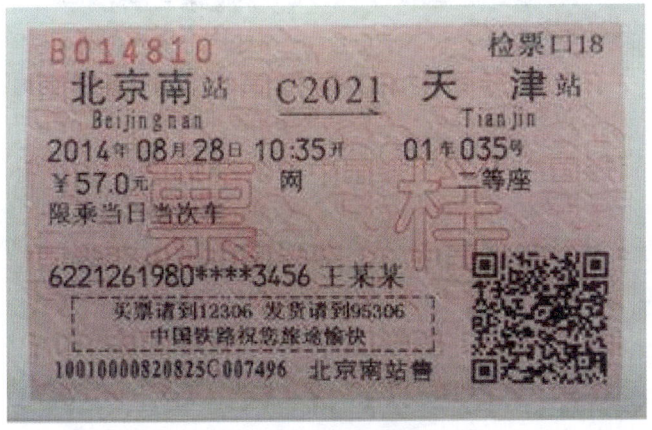

图 3-2　软纸车票

Figure 3-2　Soft Train Ticket

（2）磁介质车票。

磁介质车票如图 3-3 所示。磁介质车票，即用磁介质记录票面信息的火车票。票的正面均为浅蓝色，背面为黑色，整体手感类似塑料名片。供磁制售票机和自动售票机使用。

(2) Magnetic medium train ticket.

As illustrated in Figure 3-3, it is the train ticket using magnetic medium to record information, the front is light blue and back is black, and it feels like plastic name card. It is used in magnetic and automatic ticket printers.

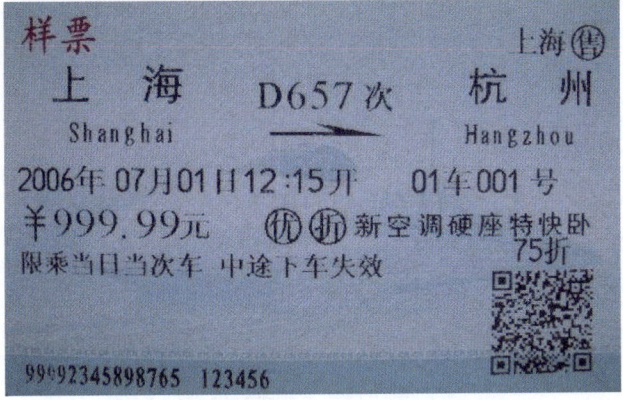

图 3-3　磁介质车票

Figure 3-3　Magnetic Medium Train Ticket

（3）列车移动补票。

列车移动补票如图3-4所示，是列车移动补票机出具的车票。

（3）Mobile ticket compensation after boarding.

As illustrated in Figure 3-4, it is printed by mobile ticket compensation printer.

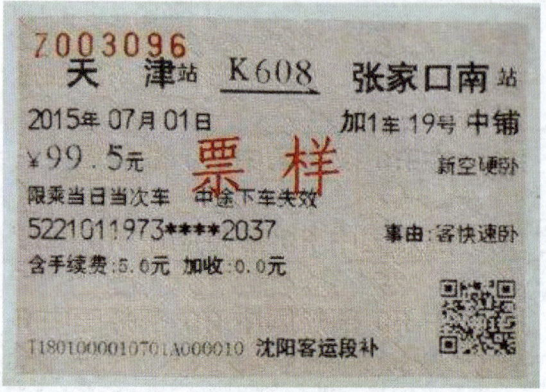

图3-4 列车移动补票

Figure 3-4 Mobile Ticket Compensation on Train

（4）代用票。

代用票如图3-5所示，是车站在计算机售票系统故障以及办理团体旅客票、包车及旅行变更和在列车内补收票价（未备有列车移动售票机）时使用的一种票据。

（4）Substituting ticket.

Substituting ticket, as shown in figure 3-5, is ticket used in case of computer ticket selling system error, and dealing with group tickets, chartered train, travel plan change, and ticket fare compensation in the train (no mobile ticket selling machine in train).

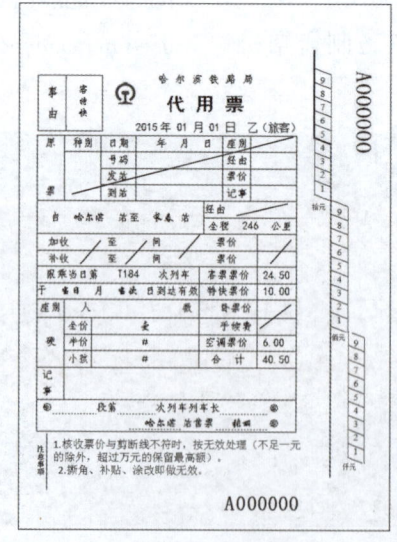

图3-5 代用票

Figure 3-5 Substituting Ticket

（5）电子客票。

电子客票，是指购票人通过中国铁路客户服务中心网订购车票之后，仅凭自己订购车票的有效二代身份证件直接到车站，通过自动检票机进站检票、乘车、出站检票的无形车票。

（6）全价票。

按票价全价发售的车票。

（7）儿童优惠票。

对符合优惠条件的儿童，按规定发售的优惠车票。

（8）学生优惠票。

对符合优惠条件的学生，按规定发售的优惠车票。学生票可享受动车组列车二等座票价优惠。动车组列车学生票票价按二等座公布票价的75%计算。

（9）伤残军人半价票。

对符合优惠条件的伤残军人，按规定发售的半价车票。

（10）团体优惠票。

对符合优惠条件的乘车团体，按规定发售的优惠车票。

知识点二：车票的票价及有效期

1. 车票的票价

动车组列车票价计算，用给定的票价率、运价里程，根据车厢等级不同，按不同公式计算。

（1）二等座票价公式。

（5）Electronic train ticket.

Electronic ticket is is invisible and used by effective ID card of the passenger after booking on China Railway Customer Service Center. ID card is used for checking in, train taking and checking out.

（6）Full price ticket.

The ticket is sold at full price.

（7）Child ticket.

Ticket with discount for children meeting favorable conditions.

（8）Student ticket.

Preferential ticket sold to students. Second-class coach is preferential for students with 75% discount.

（9）Half rate ticket for wounded and disabled servicemen.

It is sold to the servicemen meeting preferential conditions.

（10）Discount ticket for groups.

It is sold to groups meeting preferential conditions.

Key Point 2: Fare and Valid Period of Train Ticket

1. Fare of Train Ticket

Fare of CHR trains is calculated with given fare rate and mileage, and the formulas differ based on different classes of the coach.

（1）Fare formula of second-class seat.

票价 = 0.2805 × (1+10%) × 运价里程

(2) 一等座票价公式。

票价 = 0.3366 × (1+10%) × 运价里程

(3) 软卧票价公式。

上铺票价 = 0.3366 × (1+10%) × 1.6 × 运价里程

下铺票价 = 0.3366 × (1+10%) × 1.8 × 运价里程

(4) 高级软卧票价公式。

上铺票价 = 0.3366 × (1+10%) × 3.2 × 运价里程

下铺票价 = 0.3366 × (1+10%) × 3.6 × 运价里程

(5) 动车组折扣规定。

动车组票价可按公布票价打折，但应符合以下条件：

① 根据不同区域、不同季节、不同时段的市场需求，实行不同形式的打折票价。

② 二等座公布票价打折后，不得低于相同运价里程的新空调软座票价。在短途公布票价低于新空调软座票价时，按公布票价实行。70 千米及以下运价里程的动车组不进行任何形式的打折优惠，一律按公布票价执行。

③ 经过相同径路、相同站间、相同时段，不同车次应执行同一票价。

④ 同一车次，各经停站的票价在里

Fare = 0.2805*(1+10%)*fare mileage

(2) Fare formula of first-class seat.

Fare = 0.3366*(1+10%)*fare mileage

(3) Soft berth fare formula.

Upper berth fare = 0.3366*(1+10%)*1.6*fare mileage

Lower berth fare = 0.3366*(1+10%)*1.8*fare mileage

(4) Fare formula of high-class soft berth.

Upper berth fare = 0.3366*(1+10%)*3.2*fare mileage

Lower berth fare = 0.3366*(1+10%)*3.6*fare mileage

(5) Discount rules of CHR ticket fare.

Ticket of CHR trains can be discounted on meeting the following conditions:

① Different discounts based on market demand in different districts, seasons and periods.

② Ticket fare of CHR trains shall not be lower than that of the soft seat of new air conditioning training with the same fare mileage. When the publicized fare of short distance is lower than that of the soft seat of new air conditioning trains, the publicized fare is feasible. There is no any discount for the fare mileage shorter than 70km (included), publicized fare is feasible in this case.

③ Tickets fare for different routes passing the same lines and sections at the same period shall be the same.

④ Fare of the same route at the stations shall not drop away from the mileage.

程上不能倒挂。

⑤ 一等座车与二等座车的比价在 1：1.2～1：1.25之间。

2. 车票有效期

车票即为铁路旅客运输合同。任何一种合同都有一定的时效，作为运输合同的车票也不例外。其时效即为有效期间，从售出车票时起成立，至按票面规定运输结束旅客出站时止，为合同履行完毕。旅客运输的运送期间自检票进站起至到站出站时止计算。

⑤ Price ratio of the first and second class seat shall be between 1：1.2 ~ 1：1.25.

2. Valid Period of Train Ticket

Train ticket is railway passenger transit contract. There is valid period for any contract and so is train ticket. The valid period of train ticket starts from the selling of ticket and ends on completion of passenger transit. Transit period lasts from the check-in to check-out.

学习笔记
Study Notes

模块三　课堂练习 　　　　　　Module 3　In-class Exercises

问题1：识别下图车票票面信息。　　Question 1：Recognize the following ticket information.

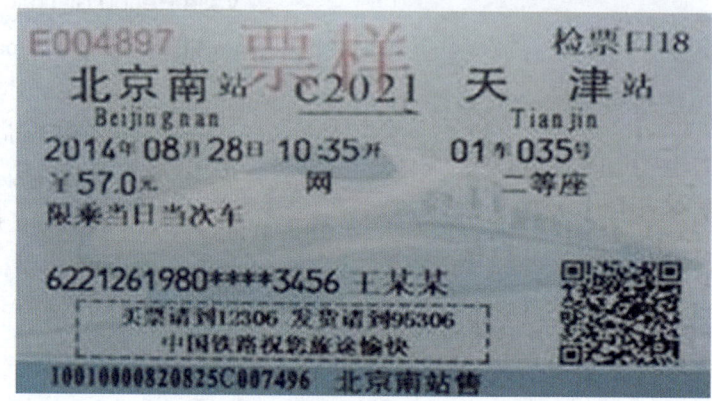

图 3-6　车票

Figure 3-6　Ticket

问题2：请计算运价里程1217千米的动车组二等座票价。　　Question 2：Calculate the ticket fare of the second-class CHR train with the fare mileage of 1217 km.

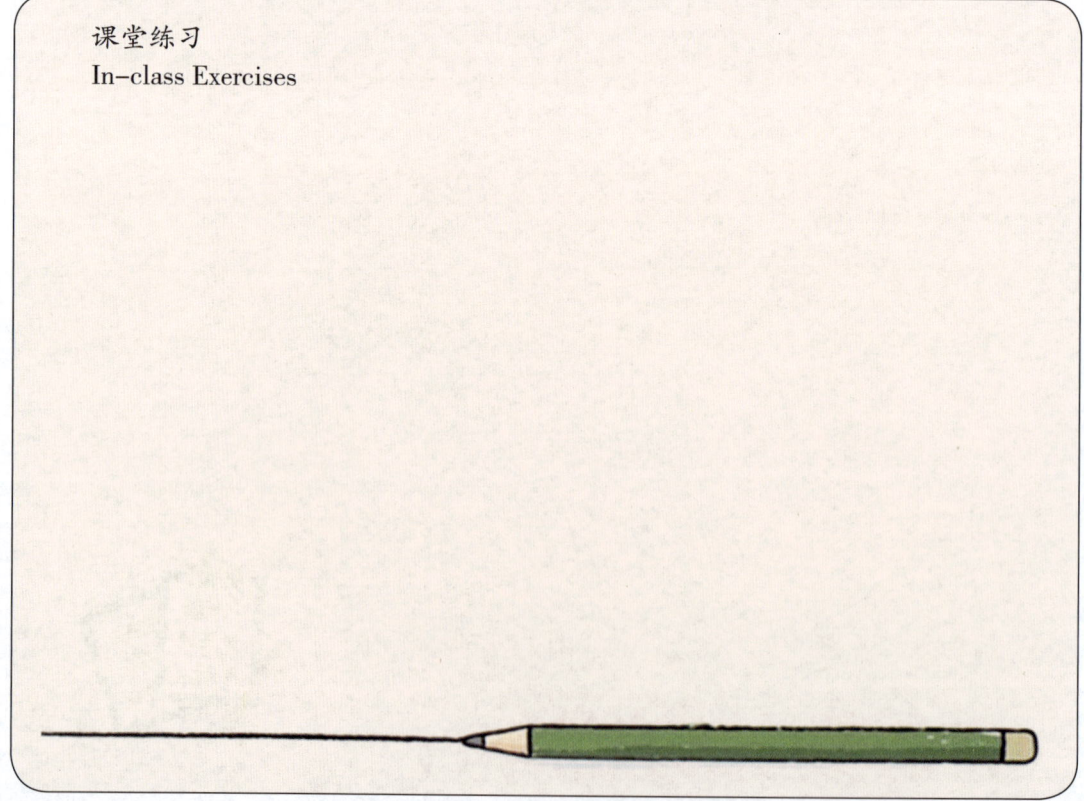

模块四 课后拓展

根据以上相关知识,学生分组讨论高速铁路车票的种类及票价计算方法。

Module 4　After-class Activity

Discuss types and calculating methods of high speed railway ticket fares in groups base on the above-mentioned knowledge.

After-class Activity

任务二 窗口人工售票

Task 2　Manual Ticket Selling at the Ticket Office

模块一　学前准备

Module 1　Preparation before Class

回忆自己在车站窗口购票、改签、退票的经历,并叙述相应的流程。

Recall your own experience of buying, rescheduling and refunding ticket at the ticket office, and state the procedures.

课前学习笔记
Study Notes before Class

模块二　课堂学习

知识点一：人工售票

窗口人工售票可以完成售票、签证、退票、取票、查询等工作。

1. 实名制售票的有效证件

实名制售票时，旅客须凭乘车人有效身份证件购买车票，并持车票及购票时所使用的乘车人本人有效身份证件原件进站、乘车，但免费乘车的儿童及持儿童票的儿童除外。

2. 动车组车票的发售规定

（1）在有运输能力的情况下，车站应根据旅客指定的到站、座别、径路发售车票；动车组列车车票最远只发售至本次列车终点站。

（2）旅客乘什么车买什么票，按票面载明的日期、车次、席别乘车，并在票面规定的有效期内到达到站。旅客乘坐动车组列车如中途下车，未乘区间车票失效。

（3）动车组列车车票当日当次有效。

（4）持有各种铁路软席乘车证的铁路员工可乘坐动车组一等车，持各种铁路硬座乘车证的铁路职工可乘坐二等车，但应当办理签证后乘车。

Module 2　In-class Learning

Key Point 1: Manual Ticketing

Ticket selling, noting, refunding, picking and inquiring can be done at the ticket office.

1. Valid Documentation of Real-name Ticket Selling

Passengers buy ticket with valid ID documentation under real-name system, and check in and take trains with the documentation used in ticket buying. Children free of charge or with children's ticket are exceptional.

2. Ticket Selling Regulations of CHR Trains

（1）Tickets shall be selling on passengers' demand for destinations, seat classes and route with adequate transit capacity. The longest distance of CHR trains is to the destination of the route.

（2）Passengers shall take trains according to the date, train number, seat class specified on the ticket and arrive at the station within the designated period. In case the passenger gets off the train in midway, the ticket is invalid for the in-taken distance.

（3）Ticket for CHR trains is only valid on the specified date and train number.

（4）Railway employee with soft seat boarding card can take the first-class seat, after registration, and those with hard seat boarding card can take second-class seat.

3. 人工签证

旅客购票后如不能按票面指定的日期和车次乘车时,应当在票面指定的日期、车次开车前办理一次提前或推迟乘车签证手续(往返票、联程票不办理改签),特殊情况经站长同意可在开车后2小时内办理。持动车组列车车票的旅客改乘当日其他动车组列车时不受开车后2小时内限制。团体旅客不应晚于开车前48小时办理改签。往返票、联程票不办理改签。

4. 人工退票

旅客要求退票时,需在票面载明的开车时间前到车站办理,退还全部票价,核收退票费。特殊情况经购票地车站或票面乘车站站长同意的,可在开车后2小时内办理。团体旅客不晚于开车前48小时。原票使用现金购票的,应按票款退还现金。原票在铁路售票窗口使用银行卡购票或者在12306.cn网站使用在线支付工具购票的,按发卡银行或在线支付工具相关规定,应退票款在规定时间退回原购票时所使用的银行卡或在线支付工具。

知识点二:窗口售票设备及操作

1. 窗口售票设备

窗口人工售票设备主要有三角牌、

3. Manual Registration

In case the passenger fails to take train on specified date and train number, he shall register to take train in advance or afterward before train leaving (registration for round-way ticket and joint ticket is not allowed), and registration can be done within two hours after train leaves with the consent of station chief under special circumstances. Passengers with CHR train ticket transfer to other trains on the same day is not limited by the 2h regulations. Group tickets shall be registered within 48h before train leaving, and registration for round-way and joint ticket is not allowed.

4. Manual Refunding

Ticket refunding shall be done before train leaves with the entire ticket fare and refund fee abducted. Ticket refunding can be done within 2h after train leaves with the consent of station chief at the ticket buying station or train taking station under special circumstances. Group tickets refunding shall be done at least 48h before train leaves. Cash is refunded if the ticket was bought in cash. Based on the regulations of the issuing bank or online payment tool, the fare is returned to the bank card or online paying tools if the ticket was bought on 12306.cn.

Key Point 2: Ticket Selling Equipment and Its Operation at the Ticket Window

1. Ticket Selling Equipment at the Ticket Window

Major equipment at the ticket selling

验钞机、话筒、学生证购票识别器、二维条码扫描器、二代身份证识读器、微机（含显示器、键盘）、切票机、POS机等。

（1）售票微机。

售票微机要求安装 Windows XP 等以上操作系统和铁路客票发售和预订系统软件（简称"TRS"）。

（2）切票机。

接收计算机指令，通过热转印头、碳带、票卷打印车票。切票机结构如图3-7 所示。

window is triangle plate, currency detector, microphone, students' ID reader, QR code scanner, 2nd generation ID card reader, microcomputer (monitor and keyboard), ticket cutter, POS terminal.

（1）Ticket selling microcomputer.

Operating system of WINDOWS XP or above, ticket selling and booking system software shall be installed (TRS for short).

（2）Ticket cutter.

Ticket is printed through thermal transfer print-head, carbon belt, ticket roller after receiving order from the computer. Inner structure of ticket cutter is illustrated in Figure 3-7.

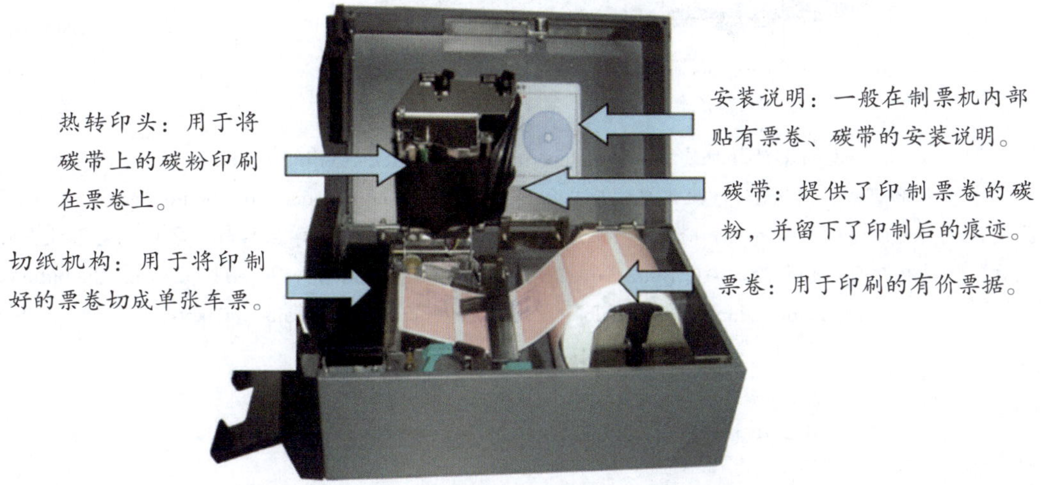

热转印头：用于将碳带上的碳粉印刷在票卷上。
Thermal transfer print-head: print the carbon powder on carbon belt on the ticket roller.

切纸机构：用于将印制好的票卷切成单张车票。
Paper cutter: cutter the printed ticket roller into single ticket.

安装说明：一般在制票机内部贴有票卷、碳带的安装说明。
Installation introduction: installation introduction to ticket roller and carbon belt is printed inside the machine.

碳带：提供了印制票卷的碳粉，并留下了印制后的痕迹。
Carbon belt: providing carbon powder and leave the printed trace.

票卷：用于印刷的有价票据。Ticket roller: ticket with price for printing.

图 3-7 切票机结构

Figure 3-7　Structure of Ticket Cutter

（3）学生优惠卡识读器。

通过感应区自动读取学生优惠卡信息，自动或手工扣减或增加学生购票次数，实现学生票的规范管理。学生优惠卡识读器结构如图3-8所示。

(3) Students' discounting card reader. Automatic reading of students' discounting card and automatic or manual reduction of ticket purchasing times for standard regulation of students' ticket. Structure of students' discounting card reader is illustrated in Figure 3-8.

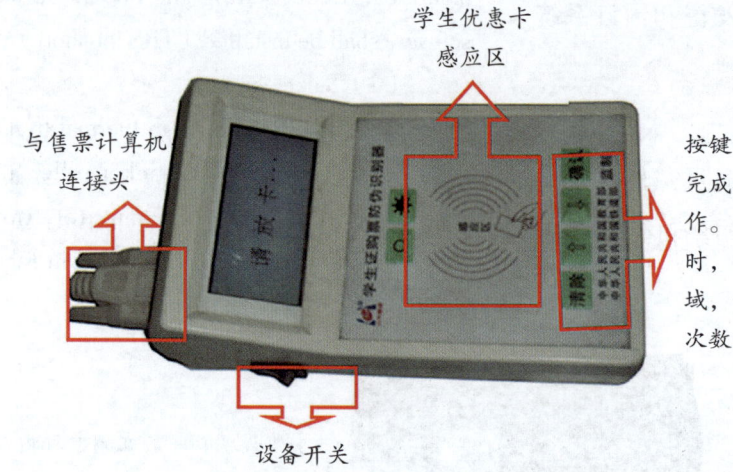

与售票计算机连接头：connecting port with ticket selling computer
设备开关：switch　学生优惠卡感应区：sensing area of students' discounting card
按键区域：可以通过按键完成扣除优惠卡次数的操作。售票窗口发售学生票时，学生优惠卡放在此区域，售票程序会自动扣除次数。Button area：discounting times can be reduced by pressing the buttons. Automatic reduction can be done at the windows selling students' tickets.

图3-8　学生优惠卡识读器结构

Figure 3-8　Structure of Students' Discounting Card Reader

（4）二代身份证识读器。

通过感应区自动读取旅客二代身份证信息。二代身份证识读器结构如图3-9所示。

(4) Second generation ID card reader.

Automatic reading of passenger ID in the sensing zone. The structure is illustrated in Figure 3-9.

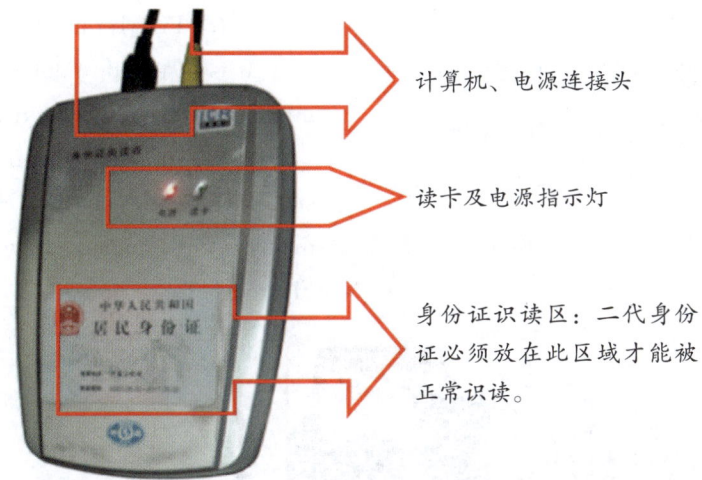

计算机、电源连接头：computer and power source connecting port
读卡及电源指示灯：card reading and power source indicating light
身份证识读区：二代身份证必须放在此区域才能被正常识读。ID card reading zone：ID card can be read correctly within the zone.

图 3-9　二代身份证识读器结构
Figure 3-9　Structure of Second Generation ID Reader

（5）二维码扫描器。

通过扫描车票右下角的二维码，还原车票信息，从而实现车票的改签、退票、验票等功能。二维码扫描器结构如图 3-10 所示。

（5）QR Code Scanner.

Ticket information is restored by scanning the QR code on the lower right corner for ticket transfer, refunding and checking. Structure of the scanner is illustrated in Figure 3-10.

图 3-10　二维码扫描器结构
Figure 3-10　Structure of QR Code Scanner

（6）POS 机。

安装于自助售票机、退票窗口、改签窗口及车站售票窗口。通过 POS 机可实现银行卡电子交易。POS 机组成如图 3-11 所示。

(6) POS Terminal.

It is installed in automatic ticket selling machine, ticket refunding and transfer window, and ticket selling window at the stations. Transaction by bank card is realized through POS terminal. Structure is illustrated in Figure 3-11.

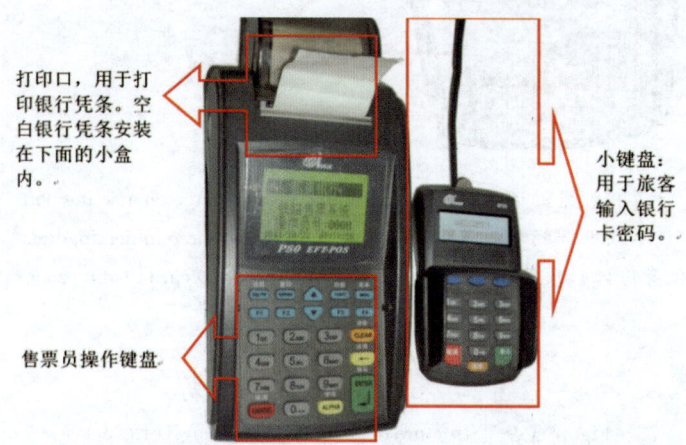

打印口：用于打印银行凭条，空白银行凭条安装在下面的小盒内。
Printing port: printing bank receipt, vacant bank receipt is put in the small box below.
小键盘：用于旅客输入银行卡密码。　Small keyboard pad: input bank password by passengers.
售票员操作键盘。　Operating keyboard by ticket selling employees.

图 3-11　POS 机组成

Figure 3-11　Structure of POS Terminal

2. 售票基本流程

发售客票基本流程如图 3-12 所示。

2. Basic Ticket Selling Procedure

Basic ticket selling procedure is illustrate in Figure 3-12.

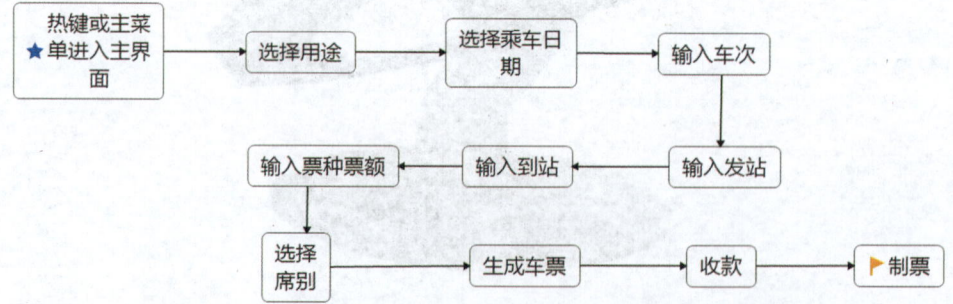

热键或主菜单进入主界面：entering main interface through hot key or main menu
选择用途：selecting function　选择乘车日期：selecting date　输入车次：inputting train number

输入发站：inputting departure station　　输入到站：input destination station
输入票种票额：input type and price of ticket　　选择席别：selecting seat class
生成车票：generating ticket　　收款：receiving money　　制票：printing ticket

图 3-12　发售客票基本流程

Figure 3-12　Basic Ticket Selling procedure

3. 售票作业操作过程　　　　　　　　　　　3. Ticket Selling Process

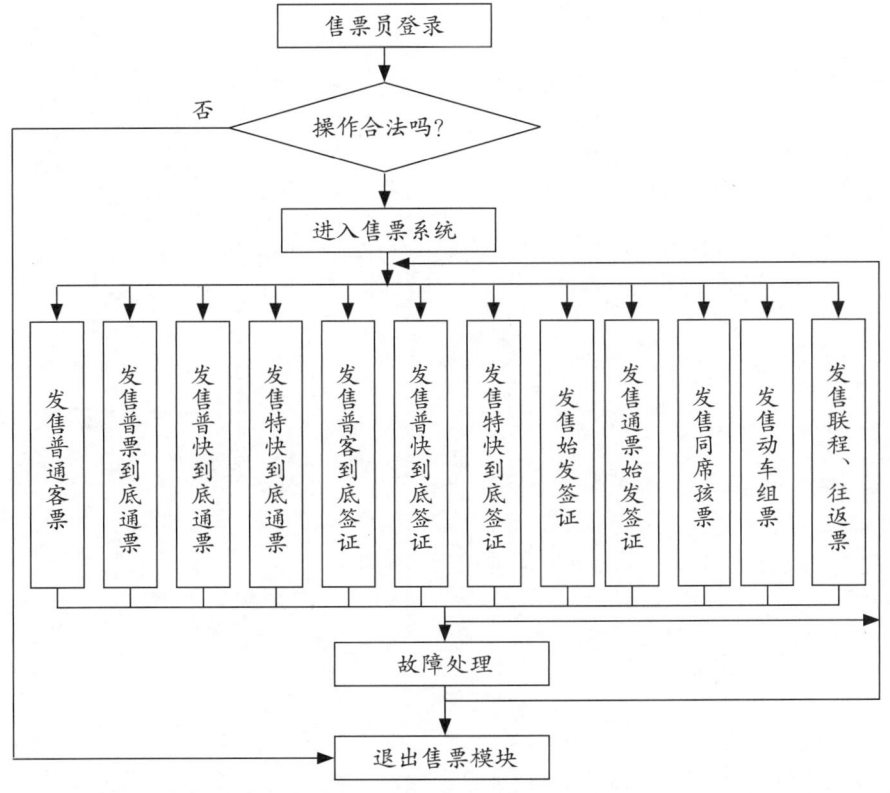

售票员登录：ticket selling employee log in　　操作合法吗：is operation rightful？
进入售票系统：enter the ticketing system　　否：no
发售普通客票：sell ordinary passenger ticket　　发售普票到底通票：sell ordinary through ticket to the end
发售普快到底通票：sale fast train through ticket to the end
发售特快到底通票：sell express train through ticket to the end
发售普客到底签证：sell ordinary passenger ticket note to the end
发售普快到底签证：sell fast train ticket note to the end
发售特快到底签证：sell express train ticket note to the end
发售始发签证：sell departure station note　　发售通票始发签证：sell ordinary ticket departure note
发售同席孩票：sell child ticket of the same class　　发售动车组票：sell CHR train ticket
发售联程、往返票：sell joint and round-way ticket　　故障处理：fault processing
退出售票模块：exiting ticket selling module

图 3-13　售票作业流程

Figure 3-13　Ticket Selling Process

学习笔记
Study Notes

模块三 课堂练习

问题：分小组运用该任务相关知识进行角色扮演，模拟现场窗口售票情景进行售票、改签和退票，落实现场处理主要环节。各小组派代表进行总结汇报，小组互评，教师点评。

Module 3 In-class Exercises

Question: role play with the knowledge related to the tasks in groups, finish tasks of ticket selling, transfer and refund at the ticket selling window. Practice the main procedures and make presentation with representatives of each group with group mutual remark and teachers' remark.

课堂练习
In-class Exercises

模块四　课后拓展

查询相关资料，小组讨论：购买实名制车票的有效身份证件有几种？并收集相关证件样本。

Module 4　After-class Activity

Search relative information and discuss the types of valid ID documentations in ticket buying in groups. Collect related ID samples.

任务三　自助售票

Task 3　Self-service Ticket Vending

模块一　学前准备

回忆自己自助购票、改签、退票的经历，描述可以采用哪些自助购票方式？如何操作？各有什么特点？

Module 1　Preparation before Class

Recall your own experience of self-service ticket buying, transfer and refund, and describe the ways of self-service ticket buying, their operating procedures and features.

课前学习笔记
Study Notes before Class

模块二　课堂学习

自助购票是一种新兴的购票方式，也是现代铁路交通系统正在推广的一种售票方式。它是在普及的互联网及铁路完善的自动售检票系统的基础上形成的售票方式。自助购票包括：互联网购票、电话订票及自动售票机购票。

知识点一：互联网售票

互联网售票，是指铁路通过中国铁路客户服务中心网（www.12306.cn）办理铁路电子客票的销售、改签、退票等业务，购票人使用联网的计算机和手机自主选择所购车票的售票方式。购票流程如下：

第一步：进入网页。

输入中国铁路客户服务中心网址www.12306.cn，进入网页。如果使用网上订票，必须先注册。

Module 2　In-class Exercises

Self-service ticket buying is an emerging way of ticket buying and is also being popularized in modern railway transportation system. It is the way of ticket selling on the basis of pervading Internet utilization and complete automatic ticket selling and check-in system. It includes online, telephone and automatic vending machine ticket buying.

Key Point 1：Online Ticket Selling

Online ticket selling is way to buy, transfer and refund on www.12306.cn by computer and mobile phones. The procedure is as follows：

Step 1：entering web page.

Input www.12306.cn to enter the web page, register first.

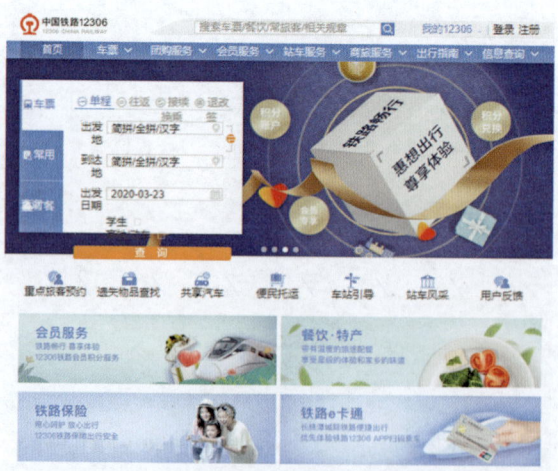

图 3-14　中国铁路客服中心网站

Figure 3-14　China Railway Customer Service Center Website

第二步：用户登录。

首次登录的用户需填写真实姓名、身份证号码、手机信息等，注册成功后需将用户名通过邮箱激活，然后重新登录才可进行网上订票业务。

Step 2：user log in.

User logging in for the first time should input real name, ID card number, telephone number and other information for registration, activate user name through e-mail, and order online ticket through re-logging in.

图 3-15　用户登录界面

Figure 3-15　User Logging in Interface

第三步：车票查询。

登录后点击页面左上角的"车票"后会出现"车票查询"项。点击后可选择出发地、目的地和日期。

Step 3：ticket inquiry.

Click "ticket" in the upper left corner and then click "ticket inquiry" to choose departure station and destination, date.

图 3-16　车票查询界面

Figure 3-16　Ticket Inquiry Interface

· 99 ·

第四步：车票预订。   Step 4：booking.

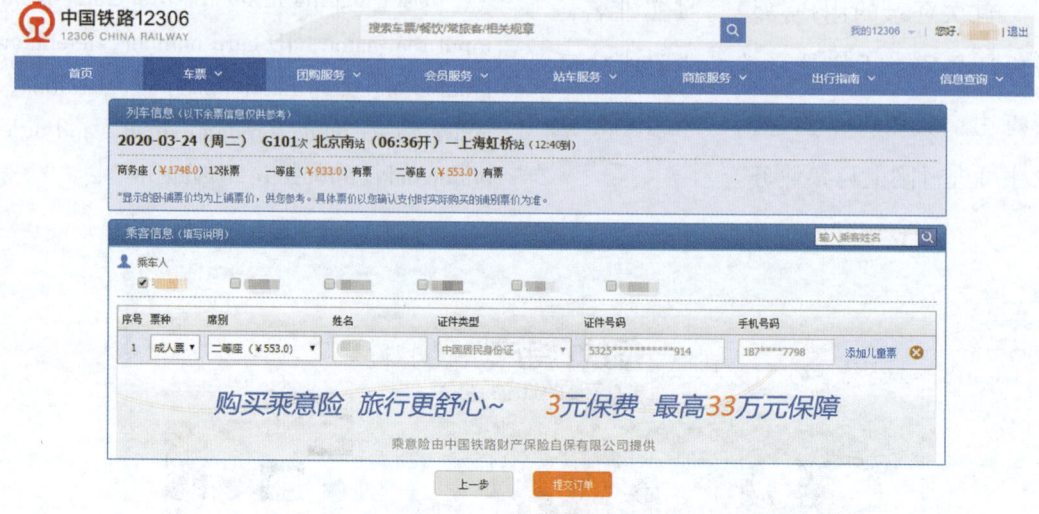

图 3-17　车票预订界面
Figure 3-17　Booking Interface

在此界面中，从常用联系人中选择或直接录入乘车人信息，也可以改签席别、票种和张数。乘车人信息填写完整后，点击"提交订单"申请车票，进入订单确认界面。

Select or input passenger information, seat class, type and number of ticket, after completing information input, clock "submit order" to enter order confirming interface.

第五步：订单确认。   Step 5：order confirming.

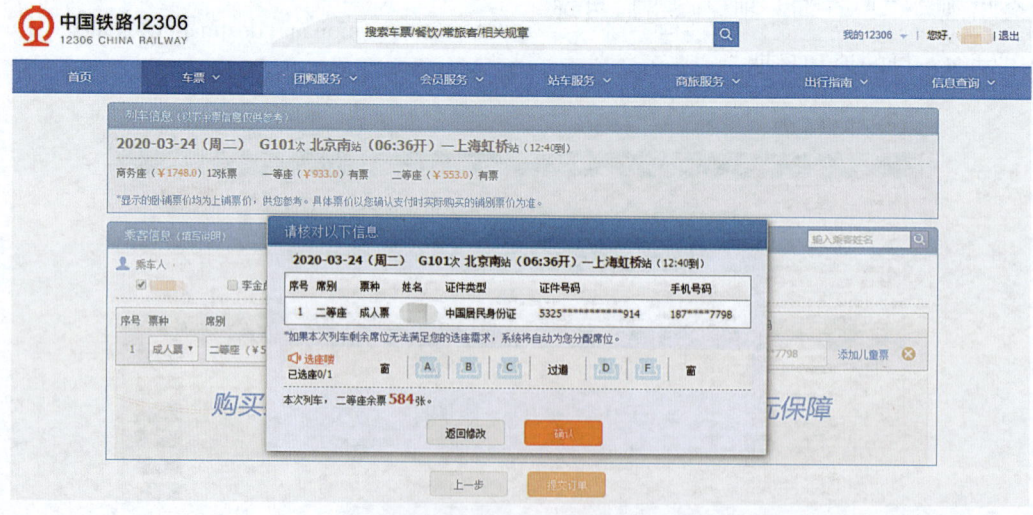

图 3-18　订单确认界面
Figure 3-18　Order Confirming Interface

旅客核对申请成功的车票信息，选择座席，确认无误后点击"确认"，进入网上银行选择界面。

第六步：网银选择。

Passenger check the applied ticket information, select seat class and click "confirm" to enter bank choosing interface.

Step 6: select e-bank.

图 3-19　订单支付界面

Figure 3-19　Paying Interface

第七步：网银支付。

Step 7: pay on e-bank.

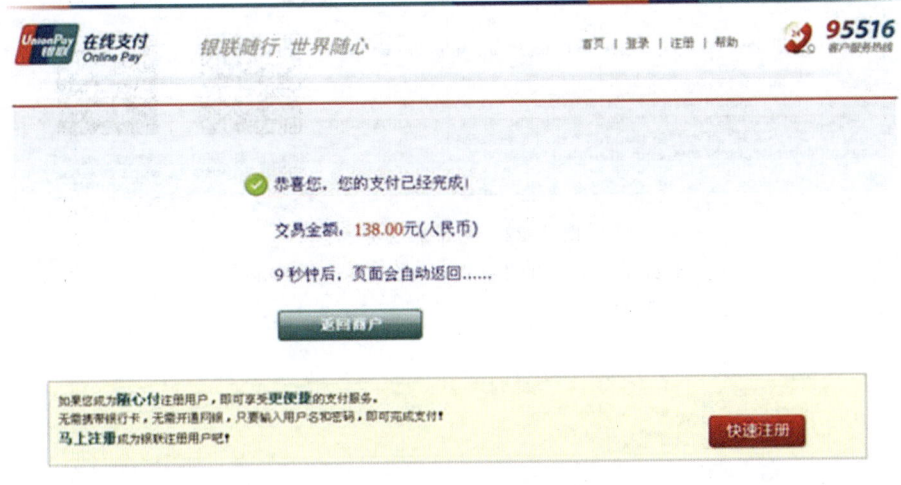

图 3-20　订单支付界面

Figure 3-20　Paying Interface

第八步：支付成功。 Step 8：pay completion.

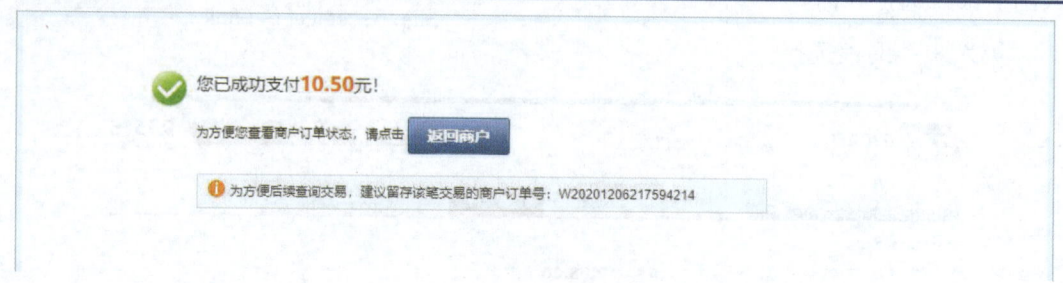

图 3–21　订单支付界面
Figure 3–21　Pay Interface

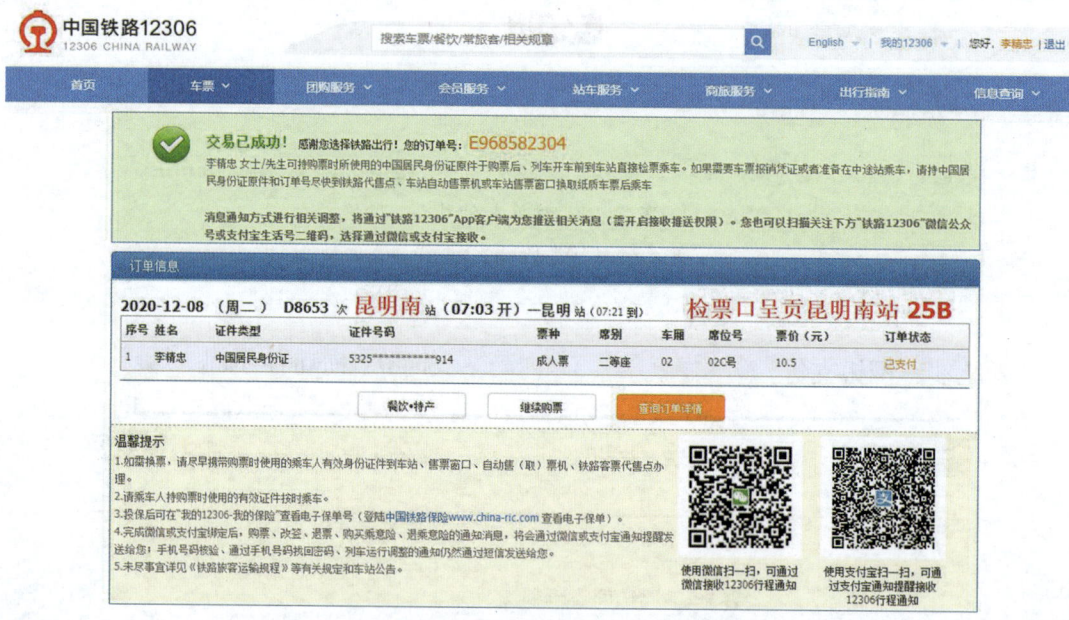

图 3–22　购票成功界面
Figure 3–22　Ticket Buying Success Interface

知识点二：电话订票

电话订票，是购票人通过拨打铁路指定订票电话号码（95105105），按语音提示，将乘车人的身份信息及所需车票的信息传入系统，订票成功后，系统播报订票单号，购票人必须记住订票单号，并在指定时间内到售票窗口或自动售票机付款、取票。否则，所订车票将被系统取消。电话订票流程如图 3-23 所示。

Key Point 2：Telephone Booking

Ticket booking by phone is to call number 95105105 and submit required information of the passenger according to voice guide and remember the order number broadcast by the system to pay for and pick ticket at the window or automatic vending machine within the designated period. The ordered ticket will be canceled otherwise. The procedure is illustrated in Figure 3-23.

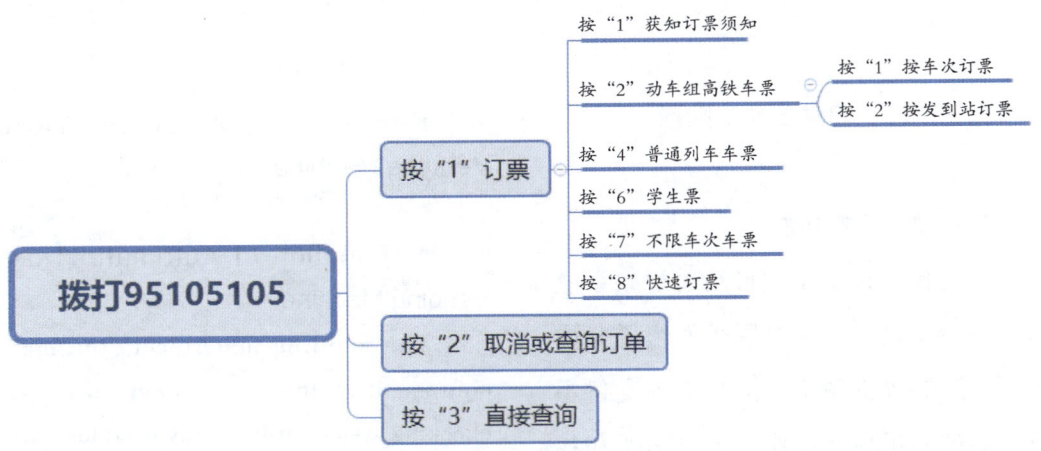

拨打 95105105：call 95105105　　按"1"订票：press 1 for ticket booking
按"1"获知订票须知：press 1 to get notes for ticket booking
按"2"动车组高铁车票：press 2 to order CHR and high speed railway ticket
按"1"按车次订票：press 1 to book by train number
按"2"按发到站订票：press 2 to book by departure station and destination
按"4"普通列车车票：press 4 for ordinary train ticket　　按"6"学生票：press 6 for student ticket
按"7"不限车次车票：press 7 for ticket without limit on train number
按"8"快速订票：press 8 for quick booking
按"2"取消或查询订单：press 2 to cancel or inquire order
按"3"直接查询：press 3 for inquiry

图 3-23　电话订票流程

Figure 3-23　Telephone Booking Procedure

购票人使用电话订票的流程为：

（1）拨打电话 95105105。

（2）输入信息。根据语音提示输入身份证信息和车次信息。

（3）记录信息。订票成功后，电话语音会播报一个 9 位数字的订票单号，购票人必须准确记录订单号。

（4）付款、取票。在规定时间内到车站或市内售票所办理付款及取票。

知识点三：自动售票机购票

1. 自动售票机功能

自动售票机是车站自动售检票系统的一个主要设备。主要用于发售磁介质车票。能够提供现金、银行卡等支付手段，通过人机界面操作，售出车票和找零。具有以下功能：

（1）自助购票。

（2）自助取票。

（3）现金支付。

（4）现金找零。

（5）银行卡支付。

（6）制票。

（7）打印凭条。

（8）凭条分类。

Ticket booking by phone procedures are as follows:

(1) Call 95105105.

(2) Input information. Input passenger's ID and train number information on voice guide.

(3) Record information. The telephone will broadcast a 9-digit order number after completion, the buyer shall record order number correctly.

(4) Pay for and pick ticket. Pay for and pick ticket in the station or ticket office within the designated period.

Key Point 3: Automatic Ticket Vending Machine

1. Function of Automatic Ticket Vending Machine

The vending machine is the major equipment in automatic ticket selling and checking system. It is mainly used for selling magnetic medium paper ticket paid by cash, bank card and so on. Ticket selling and money change is done through human-computer interface. The functions are as follows:

(1) Self-service ticket buying.

(2) Self-service ticket picking.

(3) Pay by cash.

(4) Money change.

(5) Pay by bank card.

(6) Ticket making.

(7) Receipt printing.

(8) Receipt classification.

2. 自动售票机面板组成

自动售票机面板由运营状态显示器、车票信息显示器、票款现金插入口、银行卡插入口、第二代身份证识别器、车票输出口、纸币找零口、硬币找零口等部分组成。旅客通过自动售票机面板部件的操作，完成自助购票。自动售票机面板组成如图3-24所示。

2. Panel of the Vending Machine

Panel of the vending machine consists of operating statues display, ticket information display, cash inserting port, bank card inserting part, second generation ID card reading machine, ticket output port, cash note change port, coin change note and so on. Passengers help themselves to buy tickets through operation on the panel. Components of the vending machine is illustrated in Figure 3–24.

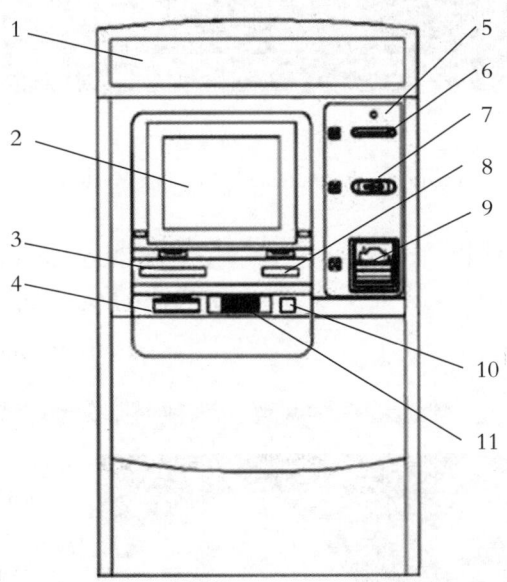

1. 运营状态显示器：operating status display　2. 车票信息显示器：ticket information display
3. 纸币找零口：cash note change port　4. 硬币找零口：coin change note　5. 召唤按钮：call button
6. 凭条口：receipt port　7. 银行卡插入口：bank card inserting port　8. 车票出口：ticket outlet
9. 票款现金插入口：cash inserting port　10. 身份证识别器：ID card reader
11. 密码键盘：password keyboard

图3-24　自动售票机面板组成
Figure 3–24　Panel Components of the Automatic Vending Machine

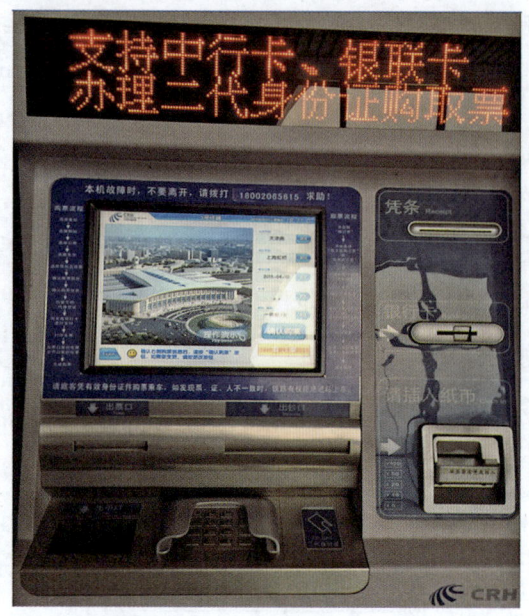

图 3-25　自动售票机
Figure 3-25　Automatic Vending Machine

3. 自动售票机操作流程

（1）初始界面。

3. Operating Procedure of Automatic Vending Machine

（1）Initial interface.

图 3-26　初始界面
Figure 3-26　Initial Interface

（2）选择发站、到站。　　　　　　　　　（2）Selecting departure station and destination.

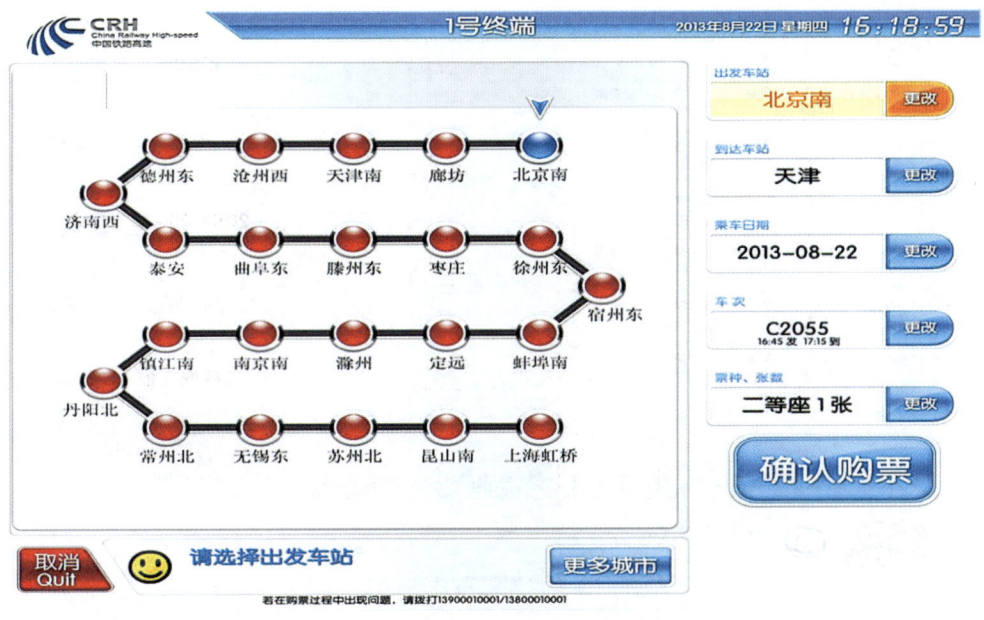

图 3-27　发站、到站选择界面
Figure 3-27　Selecting Interface

（3）选择乘车日期。　　　　　　　　　　（3）Selecting date.

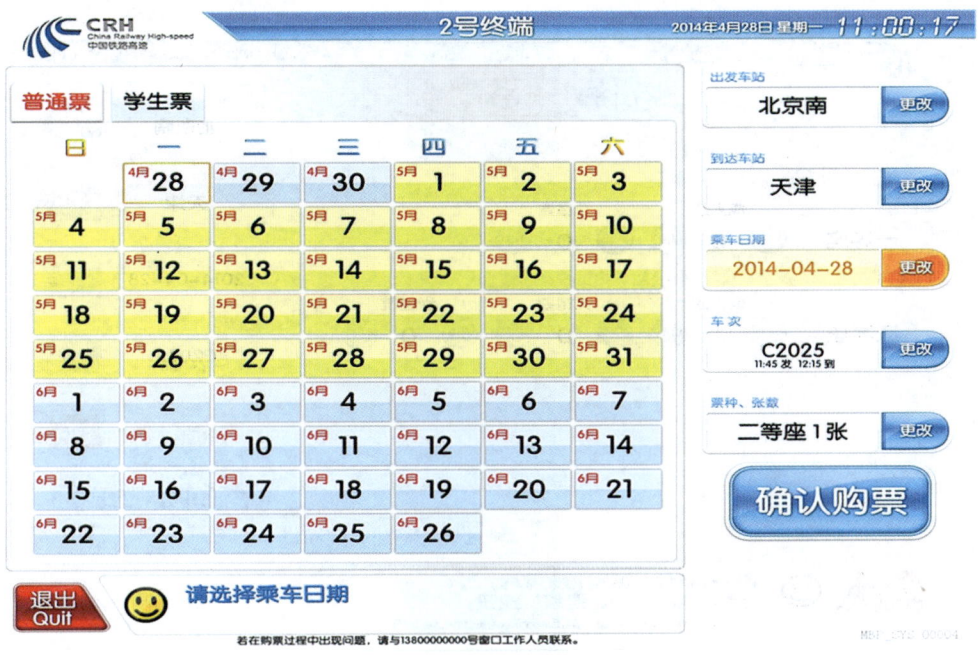

图 3-28　乘车日期选择界面
Figure 3-28　Selecting interface

·107·

（4）选择车次。　　　　　　　　　　（4）Selecting train number.

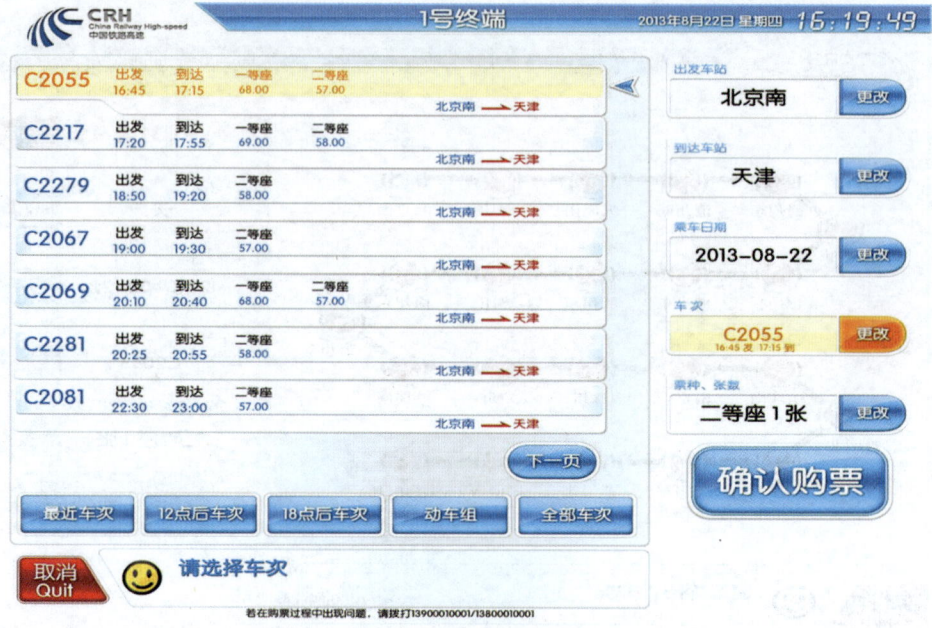

图 3-29　车次选择界面

Figure 3-29　Train Number Selecting Interface

（5）选择席别、票种、张数。　　　　（5）Selecting seat class, type and number of ticket.

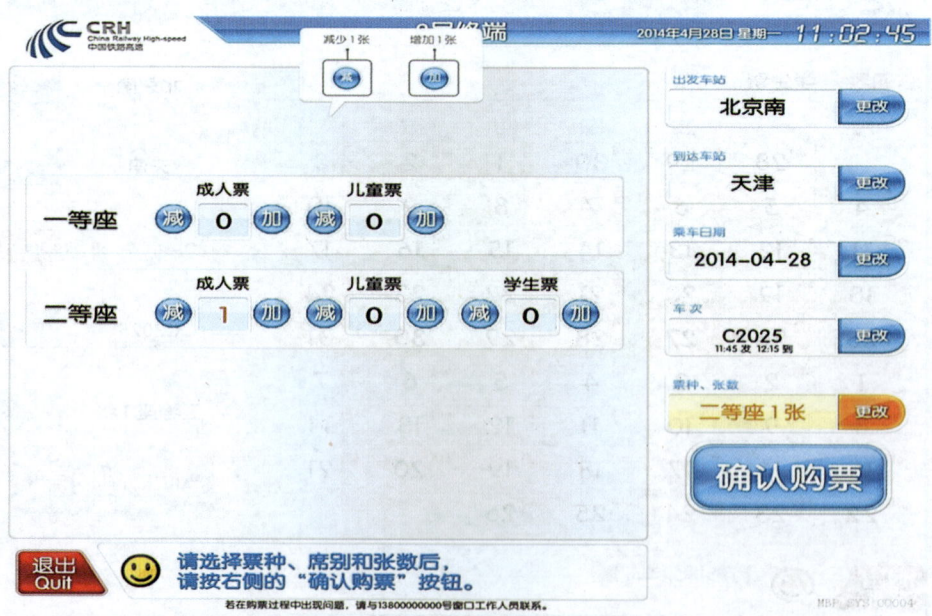

图 3-30　席别、票种、张数选择界面

Figure 3-30　Seat Class, Ticket Type and Number Selecting Interface

（6）读取身份证。　　　　　　　　　　　　（6）Reading ID card.

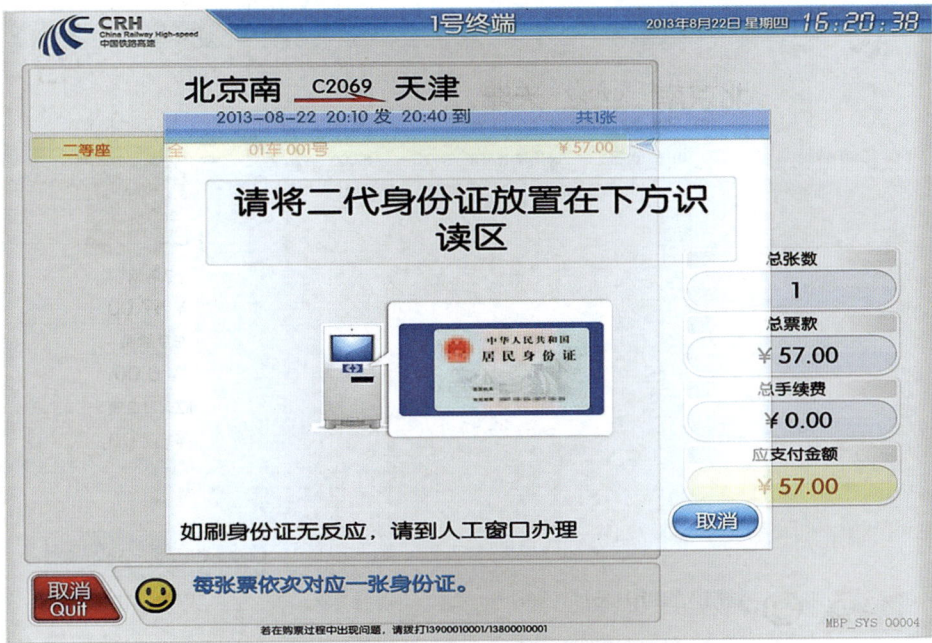

图 3-31　身份证读取界面

Figure 3-31　ID Card Reading Interface

（7）现金支付方式。　　　　　　　　　　　（7）Paying by cash.

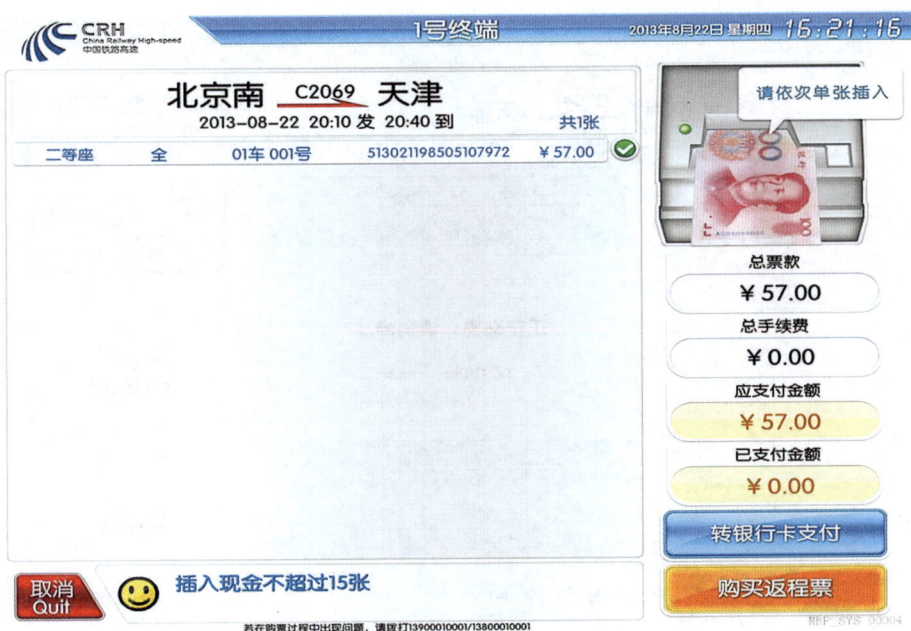

图 3-32　现金支付方式界面

Figure 3-32　Cash Paying Interface

（8）银行卡支付方式。　　　　　　　　　（8）Paying by bank card.

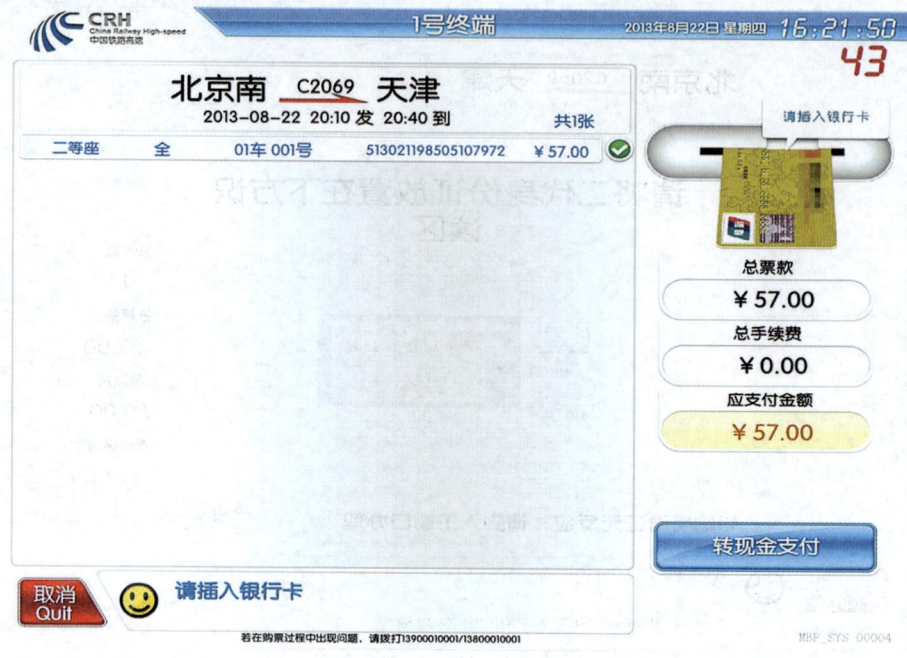

图 3-33　银行卡支付方式界面
Figure 3-33　Bank Card Paying Interface

（9）制票找零。　　　　　　　　　　　　（9）Ticket making and money change.

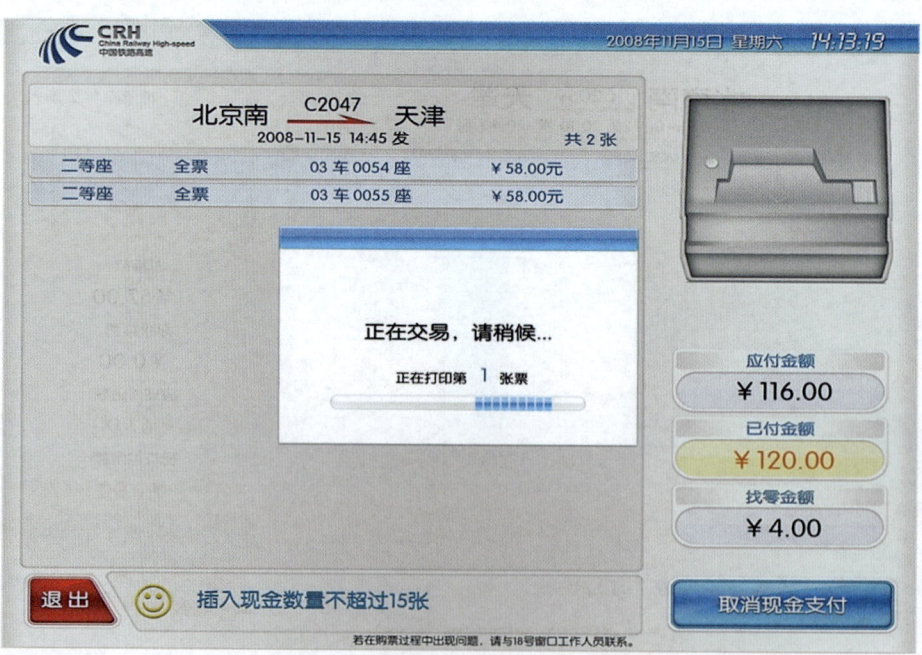

图 3-34　制票找零界面
Figure 3-34　Ticket Making and Money Change Interface

（10）提示旅客取走车票和零钱。　　（10）Reminding passengers taking ticket and money change.

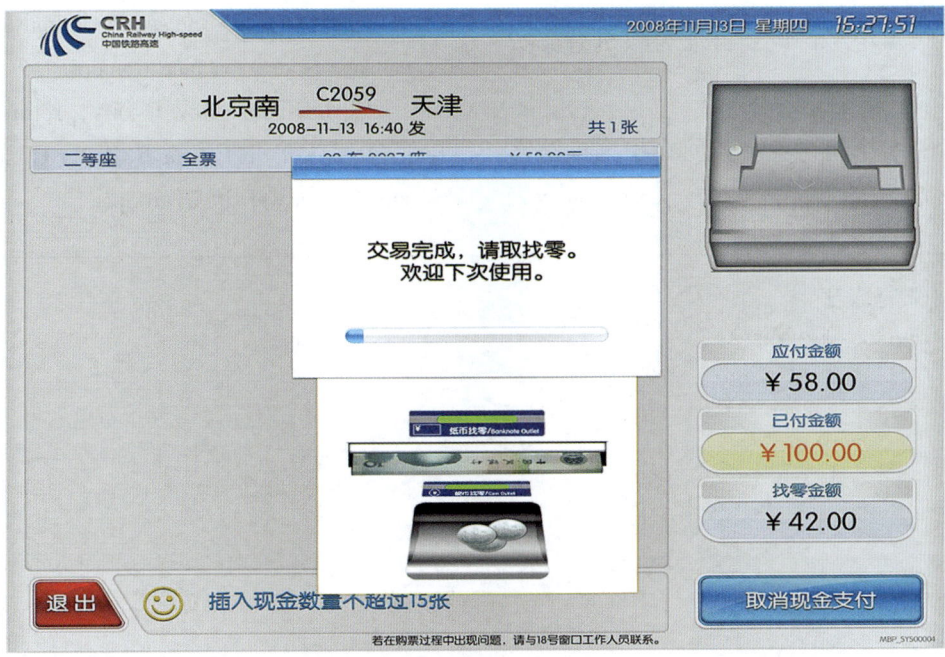

图 3-35　交易完成提示界面

Figure 3-35　Reminding Interface of Transaction Completion

学习笔记

Study Notes

模块三　课堂练习

（1）小组讨论：自动售票机有哪些优缺点？

（2）小组讨论：如何在中国铁路客户服务中心网站进行购票、退票、改签？

Module 3　In-class Exercises

（1）Discuss advantages and disadvantages of automatic vending machine in groups.

（2）Discuss how to buy, refund and transfer ticket on China Railway Customer Service Center website in groups.

课堂练习
In-class Exercises

模块四 课后拓展

查询相关资料，讨论如何使用手机APP购买车票？详述APP使用流程和常见问题。

Module 4 After-class Activity

Search information and discuss how to buy train ticket on APP in mobile phone. Discuss the procedure and common problems in using the APP.

项目四　高速铁路车站进站服务

Project 4　High Speed Railway Check-in Service

任务一　安检服务

Task 1　Security Check Service

模块一　学前准备

Module 1　Preparation before Class

高速铁路进站乘车禁止携带的物品有哪些？

What are the forbidden objects in entering high speed railway stations?

课前学习笔记
Study Notes before Class

模块二 课堂学习

知识点一：安检工作基本规范

1. 安检员职责

（1）遵守各项法律法规和各项安检规章制度，服从各级领导管理，对违反法律法规或安检规章制度的现象应制止并及时向上级报告。

（2）认真履行岗位职责，严格遵守工作纪律，不擅离职守，不做与工作无关的事情。

（3）按规定着装上岗，规范地佩戴标识，自觉维护安检人员岗位形象。

（4）熟练掌握各种安检设备的操作及识别方法。

（5）按照"逢包必检"的安检要求，负责宣传引导旅客进入安检区域。

（6）对可疑物品进行针对性探测，初步确定可疑物品性质，必要时，及时将可疑物品移交现场公安人员处理并做好记录。

（7）文明值岗，态度和蔼，遇事讲究方式、方法，做到以理服人。

2. 指挥员职责

（1）负责安检区域的安检设备及人员的管理。

（2）认真组织安检区域的安检人员按照作业流程积极主动地进行安检，确

Module 2　In-class Learning

Key Point 1：Basic Requirements for Security Check

1. Duties of Security Inspector

（1）Abide by laws and regulations, and rules regarding security check, obey leadership and management, report any violation of laws and regulations, and rules regarding security check.

（2）Perform duties carefully, strictly follow work discipline, don't leave post without permission, or do things irrelevant to work.

（3）Dress according to regulations, wear signs regularly to protect the post image.

（4）Good command of the operation and recognition method of various kinds of security check equipment.

（5）Follow the rule of check every package, and guide passenger into the check zone.

（6）Targeted detection of suspicious objects to confirm its nature, hand the suspicious object to the policeman and make record if necessary.

（7）Work with civilization and good attitude. Handle all situations in proper way to convince people by reasoning.

2. Duty of Commander

（1）Responsible for the management of security check equipment and employees.

（2）Organize the security check of passengers within the check area according to the procedures to ensure the quality and effect

保安检质量和效果。

（3）明令禁止携带的物品且不构成公安机关处理的，做好处置工作。指挥员无法处理的要及时移交现场公安人员。

（4）监督、督促值班员工按要求填写《违禁品登记簿》并做好统计和上报工作。

（5）在确保安检工作正常的前提下，合理安排安检人员的休息及用餐时间。

（6）在上岗过程中，严格执行"温馨提示"的要求。

（7）负责安排安检区域的卫生清扫工作，坚持"随脏随扫"。加强对安检区域安检人员的严格管理，认真落实各项安检工作规章制度。

3. 引导员职责

（1）在指挥员的领导下开展安检工作。

（2）对乘客携带的超长、超高、超大物品，易碎物品，易损物品等不宜机检的物品，要及时提醒手检员进行手检。

（3）引导乘客配合安检。

（4）遇特殊群体，提醒手检员进行手检。

（5）及时、准确地发现可疑人、可疑物。

4. 手检员职责

（1）在指挥员的领导下开展工作。

of check.

（3）Handle the forbidden objects properly. Hand them to the policemen on site if the commander cannot handle the situation.

（4）Supervise and urge the employees on duty to fill in "Forbidden Objects Registration Book" for calculating and reporting.

（5）Arrange employees' rest and dinning break with the prerequisite of smooth running of the work.

（6）Strict performance of Friendly Tips during work.

（7）Arrange cleaning of the checking area, insisting cleaning whenever it is dirty. Strict management of the employees to carry out working regulations and rules.

3. Duty of Guiding Employee

（1）Carry out security check under the leadership of the commander.

（2）Remind the employee to manually check the luggage with over length, over height and over size, fragile, venerable or other luggage not suitable for machinery check.

（3）Guide passengers for security check.

（4）Remind employee for manual check for special passengers.

（5）Discover suspicious people and object on time.

4. Duty of Manual Check Employee

（1）Work under the leadership of the commander.

（2）Manually check the luggage with over length, over height and over size,

（2）及时对乘客携带的超长、超高、超大物品，易碎物品、易损物品等不宜机检的物品进行手检。

（3）检查中发现可疑物品应及时向指挥员报告。

（4）负责各类安检设备的摆放及保管。

5. 操作员职责

（1）在指挥员的领导下开展安检工作。

（2）负责填写《违禁品登记簿》。

（3）熟练掌握图像识别技能，熟悉危险物品的外部特征，及时准确观察、识别可疑物。

（4）发现可疑物品，及时向指挥员报告并进行妥善处理。

（5）负责X光机、显示器、键盘的保管。

知识点二：安检工作流程

正常情况下，安检工作包含以下3项程序：

fragile, venerable or other luggage not suitable for machinery check on time.

（3）Report the suspicious object to the commander.

（4）Storage and safekeeping of security check equipment.

5. Duty of Operator

（1）Work under the leadership of the commander.

（2）Fill in "Forbidden Object Registration Book".

（3）Good command of image recognition skills and the appearance of dangerous object. Timely and accurate observing and recognition of suspicious objects.

（4）Discover suspicious object and report to the commander for proper handling.

（5）Storage of X-ray machine, monitor and keyboard.

Key Point 2: Security Check Procedure

In most case, there are three procedures for security check:

岗前准备：preparation before work　开展执勤：perform duty　任务结束：completion of task

图 4–1　安检工作流程

Figure 4–1　Security Check Procedure

1. 岗前准备

（1）集合点名：指挥员根据工作要求，集合安检员，开展点名工作，保障执勤人员全部到位。

（2）着装检查：安检员、引导员、手检员列队，指挥员开展着装检查工作。各岗位人员相互整理帽子、上衣、标识、裤子、鞋子等，发现问题进行调整。

（3）到达现场：指挥员掌控时间，要求提前20分钟到达任务现场。

（4）分配岗位：按照任务要求，按小组分配岗位，确定小组组长。

（5）传达要求：指挥员，现场叙述各岗位职责、细则、注意事项等。

（6）分配装备：以小组为单位，配发对讲机、对讲耳机、取证仪器、手持探测仪等装备。

（7）检查装备：测试、检查装备的性能，确定装备的使用分工。

2. 开展执勤

（1）文明执勤：安检各岗位人员要做到语言文明、动作文明、微笑执勤。

（2）检查安检设备：操作员提前10分钟开启安检设备，其他岗位人员配合进行安检设备性能检测。

（3）事件处置：发现不配合检查者，安检人员须立即上报组长，组长与其沟通，如无效果，上报指挥员及现场公安人员，请求指示。经检查发现对方

1. Preparation before Work

（1）Gather for attendance call: the commander gathers employees and check attendance, to ensure all employees in place based on work demand.

（2）Dress check: security check, guiding and manual check employees gather for dress check. Employees help each other to clear up cap, coat, signs, trousers, shoes and so on for necessary adjustment.

（3）Arrive on site: the commander watches the time to arrive on site 20 minutes ahead of schedule.

（4）Post allocation: divide employees in groups based on the task and name group leaders.

（5）Deliver requirement: the commander describes duties, details and notes for the posts.

（6）Equipment distribution: distribute walkies-talkie, earphone, evidence collection machine, hand detector and so on.

（7）Equipment check: test and check equipment performance, and confirm equipment allocation.

2. Perform Duty

（1）Perform duty with civilization: employees at all poss shall perform duty with smile, civilized language and gesture.

（2）Equipment check: equipment operator shall turn on equipment 10 minutes ahead of schedule, employees of other posts shall test the equipment function.

（3）Event handling: safety inspector shall report in-cooperative passenger to group leader immediately, and the group leader

携有疑似违禁物品，安检人员立即请对方配合，进行复查。对于查出的违禁物品，安检人员须按规定妥善处理。

（4）违禁物品的保管：安检人员明确告知对方，对于违禁物品铁路部门无保管和丢失赔偿义务。收缴的物品须集中存放，并做好书面记录，禁止据为己有。

3. 任务结束

（1）关闭设备：待指挥员下达停止工作命令后，各小组关闭安检设备。根据需要，做好设备断电、防雨、防盗、防破坏等保管工作。

（2）上交违禁物品：安检人员上交违禁物品，组长负责盘点，核对记录本。以小组为单位，配合指挥员，向执法部门或铁路相关部门上交违禁物品。

（3）上交装备：组长负责检查对讲机、对讲耳机、取证仪器、手持探测仪等装备的使用情况，检查无问题，上交指挥员。

（4）收队撤回：各小组进入集合地点，指挥员整队清点人数，讲评执勤工作，收队撤回。

reports it to the policemen on site, in case the communication with the in-cooperative passenger fails. Safety inspector shall re-check the suspicious object and handle it properly.

（4）Keeping forbidden objects: safety inspector shall tell inform the passenger that the confiscated forbidden objects will be stored together and the railway company is not obliged for safeguarding or loss liability. Written record shall be kept and personal possession is forbidden.

3. Task Completion

（1）Turning off equipment: all groups turn off equipment on commander's stop-work order. Equipment power-off, rain-proof, anti-theft and vandal-proof shall be done according to specific need.

（2）Hand in forbidden objects: safety inspector hands in forbidden objects to the group leader for inventory and record check. Forbidden objects are handed to law enforcement department or railway department in groups.

（3）Hand in equipment: group leader is responsible for the check of walkie-talkie, earphone, evidence collection machine, hand detector and so on, and hand them to the commander on no deflection after check.

（4）Team gathering and withdrawal: all groups enter the rally point, commander gather the team and count the team members, comment the work and return.

知识点三：安检系统

车站配有危险品检查仪、安全门、手持金属探测器等安全检查设备，对旅客及其携带品、小件寄存物品实施安全检查。

Key Point 3: Security Check System

Dangerous objects inspection tester, safety door, hand metal detector and other security check equipment are installed in stations to check passengers and their luggage, small-size deposit items and so on.

图 4-2　危险品检查仪

Figure 4-2　Dangerous Object Detection Tester

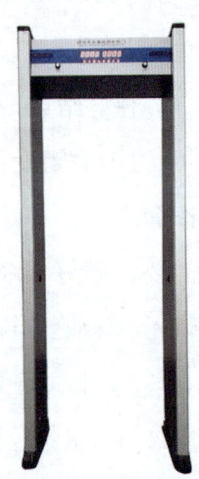

图 4-3　安全门

Figure 4-3　Safety Door

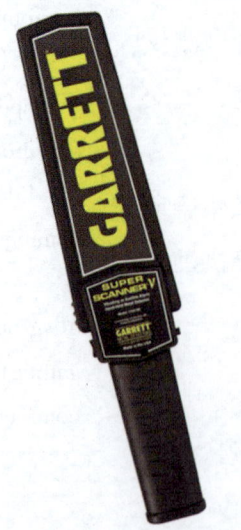

图 4-4　手持金属探测器

Figure 4-4　Hand Metal Detector

安检系统主要由X射线检查系统主机、安检操作台、传输设备等组成。

安检系统通过X射线安全检查设备，对旅行包进行安全检查，防止旅客携带容易引起爆炸、燃烧、腐蚀、毒害或有放射性的物品及枪支、管制刀具等可能危害公共安全的物品，有效地保障了铁路运输和旅客生命财产安全。

Security check system mainly consists of X-ray check system host machine, safety check operation platform, transmission equipment and so on.

Safety check system check is done through X-ray safety check equipment for the check of passengers and luggage to detect dangerous objects such as explosive, flammable, erosive, toxic and radioactive objects, guns, restricted knives and things, to effectively safeguard railway transportation, life and property security.

学习笔记
Study Notes

| 模块三　课堂练习 | Module 3　In-class Exercises |

分小组模拟安全检查过程。　　　　　　　　Simulating safety check process in groups.

模块四 课后拓展

高速铁路车站安检时查出危险品时，安检人员应该怎样处理？

Module 4 After–class Activity

How do safety inspector handle the detected dangerous objects as high speed railway stations?

After–class Activity

任务二 检票服务

Task 2　Check-in Service

模块一　学前准备

Module 1　Preparation before Class

检票时可能出现的异常情况有哪些？

What unexpected situations may occur during check-in?

课前学习笔记
Study Notes before Class

模块二 课堂学习

检票作业以自动检票机为主,人工检票为辅,同时加强检票前组队宣传和自动检票机使用方法介绍,满足旅客快速进站的需求。若自动检票机出现故障,不能运作,应及时利用剪票剪子为旅客剪票,避免耽误旅客乘车,并在事后通知维修人员进行处理。

知识点一:自动检票机检票

自动检票机

闸机的数量与布局应当与车站设施设备相协调。使用自动检票机的车站应同时留有人工通道。车站应加强进出站通道、站台的封闭管理,防止无票人员上车。

Module 2　In-class Exercises

Check-in is mainly done by automatic check-in machine, and supplemented by manual check-in. Queuing up and introduction to the use of automatic check-in machine before entering station help to speed up check-in process. In case of automatic machine failure, manual punching of ticket is required for check-in and repair employees shall be informed for repairing.

Key Point 1: Automatic Check-in Machine

Automatic Check-in Machine

Number and distribution of of gate machine shall be coordinating with other equipment in the station. Manual gate shall be kept. Exiting passageway and enclosed management shall be enhanced to prevent passenger boarding without valid ticket.

图 4-5　自动检票机
Figure 4-5　Automatic Check-in Machine

自动检票机应保证每分钟至少15人的通过能力，处理每张磁介质车票的时间不超过1秒，卡票率小于11000，通行检测最小间隔不超过200毫米。

自动检票机将车站分为付费区和非付费区。旅客在进入和离开付费区时，自动检票机对车票的有效性进行检查，给持有效车票的旅客放行，阻挡持无效车票的旅客。

（1）自动检票机的结构与功能。

Passing capacity of the gate shall be 15 persons per minute at least, and processing duration of each magnetic ticket shall be less than 1s, and ticket stuck probability shall be lower than 11000, and lowest testing interval no longer than 200 mm.

Automatic check-in machines divide the station into paying and non paying area. The machine will check the ticket validity when passenger entering the paying area to discharge passengers with valid ticket and stop those with invalid ticket.

（1）Structure and function of automatic check-in machine.

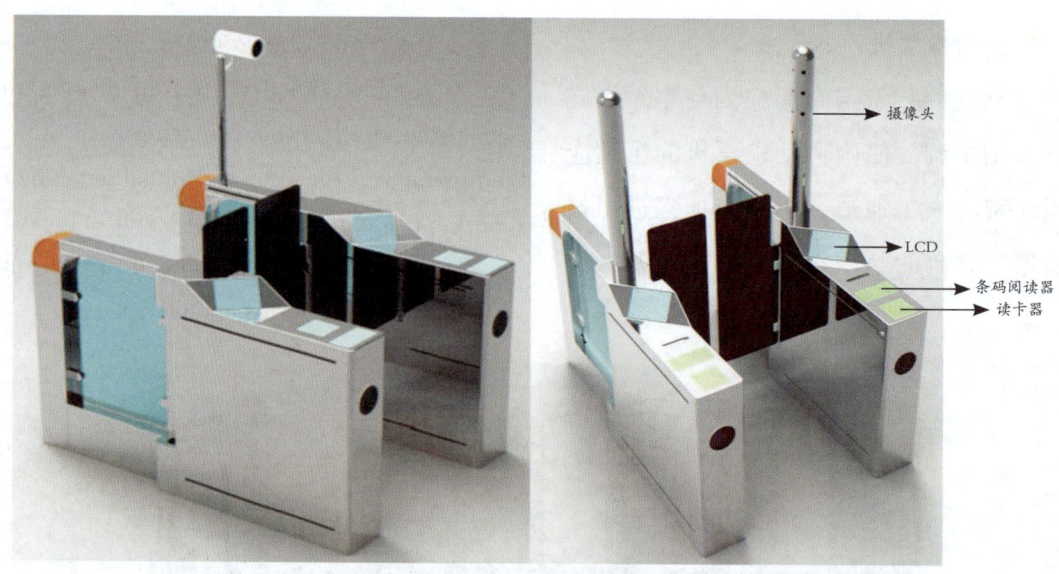

图 4-6 自动检票机结构

Figure 4-6 Structure of Automatic Check-in Machine

自动检票机由机外壳、主控单元、门控制单元、读写器、旅客显示器、方向指示器、警示灯与通过指示灯、通道传感器、扇门、维修面板、电源等部件组成。自动检票机构成如图4-6所示。

The machine consists of shell, host control unit, door control unit, reader, passenger display, direction indicator, warning light, passing indicating light, passageway sensor, door, repair panel, power source and so on. The structure is illustrated in Figure 4-6.

① 方向指示器，用绿色箭头或红色叉子分别表示自动检票机能够正常使用和不能使用，并表示能够使用时的通道方向。

② 车票入口，车票插入自动检票机的入口，供自动检票机检验车票是否有效。

③ 乘客显示器，置于机器上端表面，通过文字显示的引导信息，向乘客及客运员提供运行状态和车票处理结果。

④ 闸门开通或关闭，允许或阻止旅客进入站台乘车。

⑤ 车票出口，车票经自动检票机检验为有效票后，送出车票的出口。

⑥ 警示灯与通过指示灯，红色、绿色、黄色的警示灯，安装在机器顶部。红色灯亮表示车票无效或旅客侵入自动检票机检测范围内；绿色灯亮表示车票有效，准许旅客通过自动检票机；黄色灯亮表示车票有效，但车票为减价票（提醒客运员检查减价证明），准许旅客通过自动检票机。

⑦ 主控单元，运行机的控制软件，完成车票处理、数据通信、下载处理、状态监控等功能，采用模块化设计。协调控制设备各外围模块实现读卡、检票、车票回收、保存车票交易记录和审计数据等功能，采用以太网接口与 SC 进行通信，可以执行 SC 下发的命令、保存 SC 下发的设备参数和运行参数、向 SC 上传各种交易和审计数据、故障日志及其他信息。

① Direction indicator, green arrow and red cross is used to indicate normal and abnormal function of the machine, and show the passageway direction.

② Ticket entrance, the ticket is inserted into the entrance in the machine to check its validity.

③ Passenger display is on the upper surface of the machine to provide passengers and passenger service employee with running status and ticket processing outcome.

④ Passage gate is open or closed to permit or stop passenger entering station.

⑤ Ticket exit sends ticket out after checking the validity of ticket.

⑥ Red, green and yellow warning and indicating light is installed on top of the machine. Red light means invalid ticket or passenger invading the self-detecting range of the machine; green means valid ticket and permission of passing; yellow means valid and discounted ticket (reminding staff to check discount certificate), and permission of passing.

⑦ Host control unit is the controlling software of the machine for ticket processing, data communication, downloading, status supervision and so on. It is designed in modules. The function is to coordinate controlling equipment and the exterior modules for card reading, ticket checking, ticket recycling, keeping ticket transaction record, data auditing and so on. Ethernet and SC is used for communication to execute order sent by SC, keeping equipment and running parameter sent by SC, uploading transaction and auditing data, error log and other information to SC.

⑧ 闸门控制单元，设计为一个独立的单元，用来控制各种类型的闸机，利用此独立的控制单元可以使闸机主控单元（MCU）无须负责管理操作闸机和感应乘客是否通过等功能，从而使得闸机能够以最快的速度处理车票，大大提高了系统的性能。

车票经车票入口进入自动检票机，当被检验的车票为有效票时，车票被送到车票出口，供旅客收回，同时警示灯与通过指示灯亮绿灯（当旅客持减价票时，亮黄灯），旅客收回车票后，闸门打开，通道开启，允许旅客通过。

车票经车票入口进入自动检票机，当被检验的车票为无效票（包括车票的日期、时间、车次、检票口地点不符合本自动检票机所检的列车车票）时，车票被退回车票入口，供旅客收回，同时警示灯与通过指示灯亮红灯，闸门关闭，阻止旅客通过。

（2）检票标识。

自动检票机采用热敏方式进行检票标识打印。进站检票采用"▶"，出站检票采用"■"。

知识点二：检票作业流程及质量标准

1. 公告时间

利用车站候车大屏和检票口屏幕，

⑧ Gate passage control unit is designed as an independent unit to control gate machine of various types. The independent unit is used to make the main control unit (MCU) not responsible for gate management and checking the passing status of passengers to get the fastest ticket processing speed of gate passage, thus greatly improving system performance.

Ticket enters automatic check-in machine and is sent out to the passenger through the exist after validity check, green warning light and passing indicating light is on (yellow light is on when detecting discount ticket), the passenger retains the ticket and gate opens for passing through.

The ticket enters automatic check-in machine, in case invalid ticket is detected (date, time, train number, check-in entrance does not comply with the information to be checked on the machine), the ticket is sent back to the passenger through the entrance. Red warning light and indicating light is on, gate is closed to stop passing.

(2) Check-in mark.

Automatic check-in machine prints check mark in thermos-sensitive way. "▶" means entrance and "■" means exit.

Key Point 2: Check-in Process and Its Quality Standard

1. Schedule Announcement

Inform passengers of train arrival times, starting time of check-in on the screen of the waiting room and check-in gate. Prompt

提前告知旅客列车正晚点信息、检票开始时间。要求显示屏及时显示车次、检票（时间）信息，状态良好。

2. 提前上岗

检票开始前五分钟上岗，检查自动检票机状态，宣传车次、到站、检票机使用方法（磁票、身份证、中铁银通卡）等，打开检票口自动门。要求上岗、宣传及时准确，广播清晰，音量适宜。

3. 重点照顾

帮扶重点旅客检票进站。发现重点旅客要及时帮扶、认真交接，对旅客礼貌得体、微笑示意。

4. 确保秩序

及时处理异常情况；发现无票旅客强行进站时，立即处理。

5. 实时宣传

检票过程中，隔三分钟进行一次宣传，及时宣传，引导后续旅客检票。

6. 停止检票

按规定时间停检，显示停检标识，及时关闭检票口自动门，引导来晚的旅客到售票处办理车票改签、退票手续。要求及时锁闭，信息显示正确及时；遇来晚的旅客，耐心解释。

display of train number, check-in (time) information and good status is required.

2. Arrive at the Post in Advance

Arrive at the post 5 minutes before check-in, check the status of machine, publicize train number, stations, ways to use check-in machine (magnetic ticket, ID card, China railway bank card) and so on. Open the automatic gate of at the check machine. Prompt and accurate arrival and publication is required with clear pronunciation and proper volume.

3. Special Care

Help special passengers check in and enter. Timely help of special passengers with proper manners and smile.

4. Keeping Order

Prompt handling of abnormal situations; deal with the situation of passenger forced entry without ticket.

5. Real-time Publication

Publicize and guide the following passengers for check-in every three minutes.

6. Stop Check-in

Stop check-in on scheduled time, and show stop sign; shut automatic check-in gate and guide the late passengers to transfer or refund. Prompt lock and accurate information display is required; patient explanation for late passengers is also required.

学习笔记
Study Notes

模块三　课堂练习

分小组模拟人工进站检票流程。

Module 3　In-class Exercises

Simulate manual check-in process in groups.

课堂练习
In-class Exercises

模块四　课后拓展

Module 4　After-class Activity

进站检票如遇异常情况应如何处理？

How to handle abnormal situations in check-in?

After-class Activity

任务三　候车服务

Task 3　Waiting Service

模块一　学前准备

Module 1　Preparation before Class

高速铁路车站候车服务包括哪些内容？

What are the service content of train waiting in high speed railway station?

课前学习笔记
Study Notes before Class

模块二 课堂学习

候车室的旅客流动性很大，车站必须为旅客创造一个良好的候车环境。候车室一般实行凭票候车的方法。较大的车站可按旅客去向设置候车室或按车次、席别、客流性质设置候车室。候车室应设有一定数量的座椅，候车室内可按需要设置少量的服务项目，如提供电视、报刊、饮水、信息发布等。

知识点一：问询服务工作

1. 内容

面向旅客，热情接待旅客问讯；接听电话，解答旅客问讯；定时与广播、售票、计划客运值班室联系，掌握列车运行、客运计划、售票组织、旅客乘降和车票票价等有关情况；及时更新自动查询系统有关信息；规章文件齐全，修改及时。

2. 作业标准

（1）有问必答，答必正确，对答有礼，态度和蔼，做到"不怠慢，不粗鲁、不急躁、不厌烦"，不说"大概、可能、也许、好像、差不多、自己看"等话语。

（2）接听电话及时，铃响不得超过三声。

（3）业务资料完整、齐全、整洁，

Module 2 In-class Learning

Passenger flow is large in the waiting room, therefore, a good waiting environment is required. Waiting room is entered by ticket. Waiting room is set according to passengers' destinations, train numbers, seat classes, nature of passenger flow in large stations. Seats of certain amount shall be equipped in the waiting room, some service can also be provided, such as TV, newspapers, drinking water, information publication and so on.

Key Point 1: Inquiry Service

1. Content

Warm reception of passenger inquiry; answering telephone inquiry; regular communication with broadcasting, ticket selling, passenger transportation planning offices to know train running, passenger transportation plan, selling organization, passenger boarding and getting off, ticket fare and other relevant information; prompt update of automatic inquiry system; complete regulations and document, prompt revision.

2. Working Standard

(1) Answer every question accurately and politely, "no neglect, no rudeness, no haste, no boredom" is required; words such as "maybe, probably, like, almost, see for yourself" are prohibited.

(2) Answer telephone within 3 rings.

(3) Complete and clear document, prompt and accurate revision; binding in books, storage in fixed places with numbers

修改及时、正确；分册装订，定位摆放，有编号，有目录，方便查阅。

知识点二：寄存服务工作

寄存处是为旅客临时保管随身携带品的场所，做好寄存工作能给上车前、下车后的旅客创造便利条件。寄存物品体积小，重量轻，存取时间集中、紧迫。为安全、正确、迅速地开展寄存工作，应设置带格的物架，对寄存物品实行分区、分堆、分线保管。寄存可分别采用自动化设备（密码箱等）与人工服务的方式，方便旅客选择。

对笨重大件的或集体旅客寄存的大批物品可堆放在一起分堆保管，易碎品应固定货位存放。在大的客运站现已采用电子技术控制的双控编码锁小件寄存柜，旅客可自己选定号码开柜，既安全又方便，为车站服务人员的管理工作创造了良好条件。寄存柜如图4-7所示。

and catalogs for reference.

Key Point 2: Luggage Deposit Service

Depository is the place for temporary deposit of passengers' luggage. It is convenient before passengers boarding and getting off the train. Deposit luggage is small and light, deposit and taking intervals are short. Shelf with separated cells is set for safe, accurate and quick deposit of luggage in piles, sections and lines. Deposit can be done automatically and manually for passengers' choice.

Large and heavy luggage, or luggages of group passengers can be put in bunches together, and fragile luggage is put in fixed place. Electronic controlled dual code lock deposit cabinet is installed in larger stations, and passengers can select number to deposit for the convenient management of the employees. The deposit cabinet is illustrated in Figure 4-7.

图 4-7 寄存柜

Figure 4-7 Deposit cabinet

知识点三：重点旅客服务工作

（1）车站进站口设立接待处（逐步覆盖到各进站口），提供预约、接待服务；站内客运员发现重点旅客后，询问旅客需求并报告接待处。接待处登记、确认后，开具重点旅客交接单（一式三联），通知服务人员到场，并通知到站安排专人接站。

（2）专人送至重点旅客候车区候车，并提供相应服务。

（3）提前办理检票进站，通过升降梯送至站台，与列车办理交接。

Key Point 3: Service for Special Passengers

（1）Reception desk is set on the station entrance (gradual installation in every passenger entrance) to provide reservation and reception service; passenger service employees ask for special passengers' need and report it to the reception desk. Passenger handover receipt (in triplicate) is issued after information is registered and confirmed, then service employee is on site and meeting employee at the destination is set.

（2）Assigned employee sends the special passenger to the waiting room and provide required service.

（3）Check-in ahead of schedule and send passenger to the platform by elevator and hand over with trains.

学习笔记
Study Notes

模块三　课堂练习

分小组模拟车站候车问询服务及重点旅客服务工作。

Module 3　In-class Exercises

Simulating inquiry and special passenger service in groups.

模块四 课后拓展

Module 4 After-class Activity

解答旅客问询的方法有哪些？

What are the ways to answer passengers' questions?

项目五　高速铁路车站站台乘降服务

Project 5　High Speed Railway Station Platform Elevator Service

任务一　站台概述
Task 1　Overview of Platform

模块一　学前准备

高速铁路车站乘客如何到达站台？

Module 1　Preparation before Class

How do high speed railway passengers arrive at the platform?

课前学习笔记
Study Notes before Class

模块二 课堂学习

知识点一：车站台内结构作用

1. 车站站台基本结构

国内主流形式的高铁站，分为三层，1层为站台，2层高架候车室跨越整个站台，地下为到达层（如图5-1）。但是也有不同的设计，比如高架站台、候车室和到达都在1层，站台在2层；或者地下站台，比如深圳福田，-1层是交流层，-2层是候车区，-3层是站台；还有深圳北的上进上出，在高铁上下都有地铁站。此外普高共站也有不同，一些改造过的车站也用了上进下出的格局，而没有改造过的车站采取普高分场，高速场上进下出，普速场沿用原来的方式，两者通过天桥或者直接在站外地道连接，甚至于没有直通连接方式。

2. 车站站台的作用

供旅客上下车，给旅客提供短暂休息空间。

Module 2　In-class Learning

Key Point 1: Structure and Function of Station Platform

1. Basic Structure of Station Platform

There are three floors of the mainstream forms in domestic high speed railway stations, the first floor is platform, high-rise waiting room on the second floor crosses the entire platform and the underground level is arrival floor (as illustrated in Figure 5-1). But there are also exceptions. High-rise platform, waiting room and arrival floor is on the first floor, platform is on the second floor; or there is underground platform, in Futian station of Shenzhen city, first floor underground is communication floor, second floor underground is waiting area and third floor underground is platform; in North Train station of Shenzhen, entrance and exit floor are both above the ground with subway stations; and there are also differences in normal speed railway stations; in some remodeled stations, entrance and exit are above the ground, and in original stations, ordinary trains is divided, entrance is above and exit is under the ground for high speed trains; overpass or underground passage is built to connect the two stations, or there is no direct connection between the two stations.

2. Function of Station Platform

The space for passenger boarding and getting-off, short break for passengers.

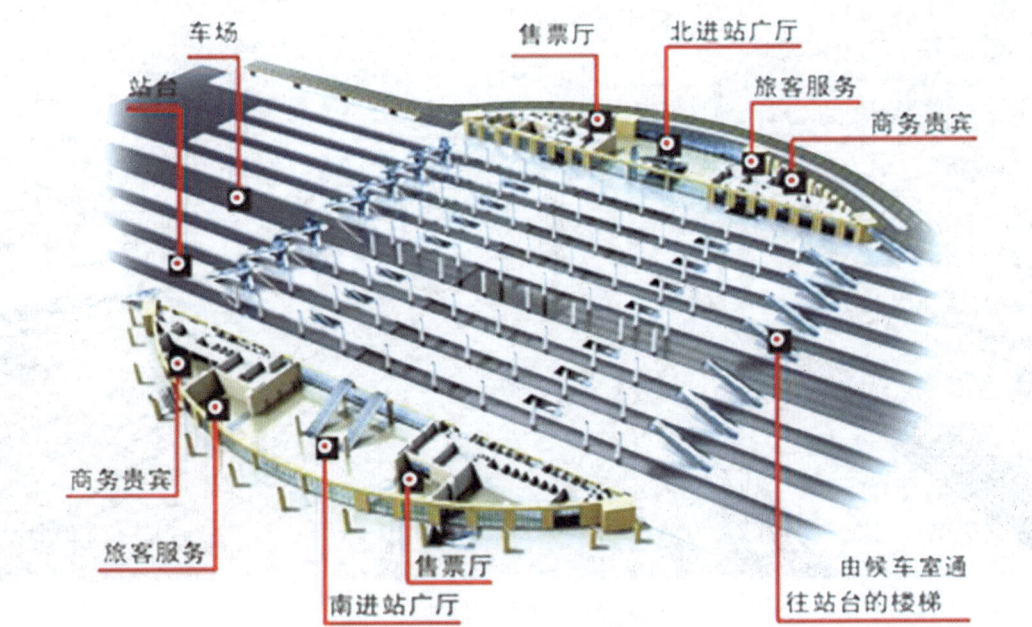

图 5-1 车站站台常见结构
Figure 5-1　Common Structure of Station Platform

图 5-2 常见高铁站台
Figure 5-2　Common High Speed Railway Station Platform

图 5-3 高铁车站站台
Figure 5-3 High Speed Railway Station Platform

知识点二：车站站台内常见设施设备

1. 车站站台黄色安全线

高铁站台离边缘 1 米处有一条黄色的安全警示线，旅客应站在安全警示线以外候车。作用是禁止旅客从候车室跨越。

2. 车站站台停车位标志

我们叫它们"地标"，即地上的标志（标识）。由于动车在车站停靠时间较短，为了到站时乘客不必拎着大包小包赶车，车站往往会在动车到站前提前让旅客进站。乘客们根据"地标"的指引，找到所购车票对应的车厢位置，即可有序排队上车。

Key Point 2：Common Equipment and Facilities in Station Platforms

1. Yellow Safety Line in Station Platform

A yellow safety line is set 1 m away from the platform edge and passengers shall stand outside the line. The function is to prevent passengers from trespassing.

2. Parking Lot Sign in Station Platform

The sign is called ground mark, namely mark (sign on the ground). CRH trains often stop for a short time on the station and passengers arrive at the platform to avoid catching trains with heavy luggage advance. With the guidance of the ground mark, passengers wait according to the coach number and board the train in order.

图 5-4 高铁车站地标

Figure 5-4 Ground Marks in High Speed Railway Stations

图 5-5 高铁车站标志

Figure 5-5 Signs in High Speed Railway Stations

模块三　课堂练习

请查查为什么要在站台设置黄色安全线（伯努利原理）。

Module 3　In-class Exercises

Consult information to understand the reason of setting yellow safety line at the platform (Bernoulli Principle).

学习笔记
Study Notes

任务二　站台客运员工作概述

Task 2　Job Description of Platform Passenger Service Employees

模块一　学前准备

假设你乘坐动车 11 点 20 分到达昆明南火车站，需要乘坐 11 点 50 分的动车从昆明南火车站出发去外地，请问你 11 点 20 分下车后准备怎么做？

Module 1　Preparation before Class

Assume that you arrive at the Kunming South Railway Station on 11：20 and leave by CHR train on 11：50, what you should do after getting off the first train on 11：20?

课前学习笔记
Study Notes before Class

模块二　课堂学习

站台客运员工作职责如下：

（1）熟知本职业务，遵章守纪，执行命令，听从指挥，坚持全面服务，重点照顾，文明礼貌地为旅客服务。

（2）按作业标准要求，组织好旅客购票、候车、进出站秩序，宣传旅行常识，搞好安全检查，负责查验车票，维护乘降秩序和解答问询。

（3）掌握列车运行情况及到、开时刻和停靠站台，按时显示车次方向牌，有秩序地组织旅客检、收票，正确统计上、下车人数。

（4）认真执行接送车制度，组织旅客通过地道、天桥、平过道口上下车，从指定出入口进出站，严禁旅客扒车、钻车、横越轨道和在列车背面上下，安全迅速地组织旅客乘降，确保旅客人身安全、列车正点。

（5）负责军用人员列车的接送，正确查验军用人员的乘车中转凭证，确保军用人员运输安全。

（6）坚守岗位，尽职尽责，严格查堵，及时清理站台，严禁闲杂人员在站内逗留，防止易燃、易爆、危险违禁品进站上车，确保旅客运输安全。

Module 2　In-class Learning

Duties of platform passenger service employees：

（1）Good command of the job duties, obey regulations and follow orders; serve all passengers and care for special guests with good manners and politeness.

（2）Organize ticket buying, waiting, entering and exiting according to working standard; publicize common travel knowledge; conduct safety check, ticket check; maintain order and answer questions.

（3）Command of train running status, schedules and platform; display training number on time; organize ticket checking and collecting; counting passenger numbers of boarding and getting off the train.

（4）Careful execution of train sending and receiving system, organize passengers boarding and getting off by underground passages, overpasses and ground passages; entering and exiting stations through certain places; prevent passengers from climbing and entering trains without permission or cross the railways, and boarding and getting off from the back of trains; safe and prompt elevating of passengers to ensure passengers' safety and train punctuality.

（5）Receiving and sending of trains taken by servicemen to check their transfer certificate to ensure their safety.

（6）Hold to the post, strict search for interception with due diligence and clear the platform on time. Prevent non staff from lingering in the station, prevent flammable, explosive and dangerous objects outside the stations to ensure safe transportation.

图 5-6 站台客运员

Figure 5-6　Passenger Service Employee at the Platform

图 5-7　站台客运员组织排队候车

Figure 5-7　Guide Passengers Queuing up for Boarding

学习笔记
Study Notes

模块三　课堂练习

（1）有旅客越过黄色安全线该如何处理？

（2）有旅客不知道去哪里候车询问你该如何处理？

Module 3　In-class Exercises

（1）How to deal with the situation of passenger trespassing the yellow safety line?

（2）How to direct passenger to the correct waiting area?

课堂练习
In-class Exercises

任务三 乘降服务与站车交接

Task 3 Elevating Service, Station and Train Handover

模块一 学前准备

遇到拿错误车票来乘车的乘客如何处理?

Module 1 Preparation before Class

How to help the passenger with wrong ticket?

课前学习笔记
Study Notes before Class

模块二 课堂学习

知识点一:乘务员出乘前准备

列车到达前 15 分钟乘务员列队由列车长带领到站台接车,在列车中部车厢列队接车,与对班班组办理交接。

(1)乘务员迅速将乘务箱按规定定位,一人负责对四节车厢的安全锤、灭火器、安全乘降梯、过渡板、耳机设备设施进行检查。

(2)检查灭火器铅封、指针、有效期。

(3)检查垃圾箱、卫生间、洗面间、座席下、行李架上、大件行李处。

(4)检查车内清扫备品、检查坐便垫、消毒条、服务指南、清洁袋、洗手

Module 2　In-class Exercise

Key Point 1:Service Employees' Preparation before Work

Head of train crew lead the team to the platform for train receiving 15 minutes before train arrives, line up in the middle coach of the train and hand over with the other crew.

(1) Attendants put their luggage box in fixed places, every attendant check safety hammers, fire extinguishers, safety elevators, interim plates, earphones in four coaches.

(2) Check the lead seal, pointer and valid date of the fire extinguisher.

(3) Check dust bins, lavatories, washing rooms, place under the seat and above the luggage shelves, place for large luggage.

(4) Check the sizing of spare cleaning

图 5-8　列车长出乘前检查

Figure 5-8　Chief Crew Check before Train Leaves

液等消耗品的配备数量和定型情况。

（5）整理头枕片、定型网袋内的杂志、服务指南、清洁袋等物品。

（6）整理、定型备品存放处物品进行分类放置。

（7）发现问题通知列车长处理。

知识点二：乘务员乘降服务要求和标准

1. 服务要求

（1）在车门内迎接旅客上车。

（2）引导旅客就座，妥善安放行李，解答旅客问询，妥善安排重点旅客，发现问题及时处理。

（3）及时劝告送客人员下车，不能处理时向列车长报告。

（4）提示并帮助旅客将大件行李安放在大件行李处。

（5）开车前5分钟，广播提醒送客人员及时下车。

（6）向列车长报告分管车厢旅客上、下情况。

（7）列车启动时，面带微笑，目视前方，行注目礼，向站台点头致意。

2. 服务标准

（1）言行规范，引导有序，妥善安排。发现问题，妥善处理，报告及时。按时播报，使用普通话，音量适宜。

equipment, number and sizing of toilet pad, sterilizing strip, service introduction, liquid soap.

(5) Clear up headrest, sizing magazines, service introduction and clear bags in the net.

(6) Clear up and sizing spare items in the deposit place.

(7) Report problems to the head of crew.

Key Point 2: Requirement and Standard of Elevating Service

1. Service Requirement

(1) Meet passengers inside the train gate.

(2) Guide passengers to the seat and put luggage properly, answer passenger's questions, proper service to special passengers and handle any possible problems on time.

(3) Advise passenger sending people to get off the train on time, report any possible problem to head chief.

(4) Remind and help passengers to put big luggage in fixed places.

(5) Remind passenger sending people get off the train 5 minutes before train departs.

(6) Report passenger boarding and getting off status in each coach.

(7) Salute with eyes and smile when the train departs and nod greeting to the platform.

2. Service Standard

(1) Standard manners and language, orderly guidance, proper arrangement and prompt report. Broadcast on time in mandarin

（2）商务座、一等座旅客较多时，乘务员在始发时要协助商务座服务员做好迎接旅客上车、引导等工作。

（3）确认到位、按时发车。

with proper volume.

（2）When passengers of business and first class are many, service employees shall assist the service employees in the business class to greet and guide the passengers.

（3）Confirm the proper position and departs on time.

图 5-9　乘务员检查车票

Figure 5-9　Employee Checking Ticket

图 5-10　乘客下车

Figure 5-10　Passengers Getting off the Train

学习笔记
Study Notes

模块三　课堂练习

（1）乘务员检查车票，发现车票不是本次列车如何处理？

（2）中间站停车，停车时间很短，有大量旅客要下车抽烟如何处理？

（3）有无票旅客要求上车补票如何处理？

Module 3　In-class Exercises

（1）How does employee deal with the situation after checking and discovers the wrong ticket?

（2）How to deal with the situation when many passengers getting off to smoke during short stopping interval?

（3）How to help passengers without ticket compensate after boarding?

课堂练习
In-class Exercises

项目六　高速铁路车站出站服务

Project 6　High Speed Railway Station Check-out Service

任务一　出站检票作业

Task 1　Check out

模块一　学前准备

Module 1　Preparation before Class

高速铁路车站出站检票作业中，可能会遇到哪些问题，导致乘客无法出站？

In the high speed railway station checking-out operations, what problem may occur and lead to the failure in check-out?

课前学习笔记
Study Notes before Class

模块二 课堂学习

知识点一：出站检票作业流程

正常情况下，出站检票作业包含以下4项程序：

Module 2　In-class Learning

Key Point 1：Check-out Procedure

In most case, there are four procedures in check-out:

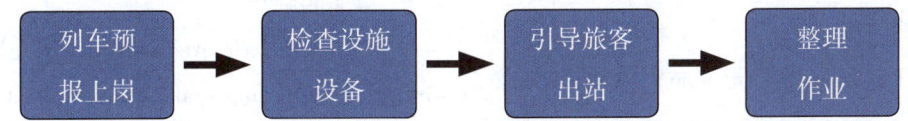

列车预报上岗：train forecast and arrive at the post　检查设施设备：equipment and facility check
引导旅客出站：guiding passengers exiting　整理作业：clear up

图 6-1　出站检票作业流程

Figure 6-1　Check-out Procedure

1. 列车预报上岗

出站检票人员在列车到达前提前到岗。

2. 检查设施设备

（1）清理出口通道，开足自动检票机，做到通道畅通，无闲杂人员和障碍物，方便旅客通行。

（2）检查出站闸机、电梯、到达显示屏、补票电脑（含票据）等设施设备，确认状态良好、显示正确。

3. 引导旅客出站

（1）在出站口面向旅客立岗，通过广播、小喇叭等提示旅客提前手持车票，宣传如何使用自动检票机，引导旅客快速、有序出站。

1. Train Forecast and Arrive at the Post

Check-out employees arrive at the post before train arrives.

2. Equipment and Facility Check

（1）Clear exit passageway, open enough automatic check out machine for smooth passing without other people and barrier.

（2）Examine check-out gate, elevator, arrival display, ticket compensation computer (including receipt) and other equipment to ensure good status and correct display.

3. Guiding Passengers Exit

（1）Stand at the exit facing the passengers, remind them to hold ticket in hands with broadcast and loudspeaker and exit with automatic check out machine for fast and orderly exit.

（2）宣传引导持软纸车票或其他乘车凭证的旅客至人工通道，做好验票出站工作。

（3）遇有无票或减价不符旅客，引导旅客到补票处办理相关手续。

4. 整理作业

（1）旅客出站完毕后，检查自动检票机、人工通道门，准备下次出站检票作业。

（2）引导出站地道内滞留人员出站。

（3）全天作业完毕，关闭出口处大门。

知识点二：特殊情况下的出站检票作业

1. 处理闸机异常

（1）发现因错误使用导致闸机报警，立即帮助旅客处理通过。

（2）持减价票的旅客通过闸机时，根据相应提示，核对旅客减价凭证。

（3）自动闸机卡票时，立即处理，并引导旅客通过其他闸机或人工检票口出站。

（4）自动闸机故障时，及时引导旅客通过其他闸机或人工检票口出站；全部故障时，改为人工检票出站。

2. 办理旅客到补

（1）旅客铁路乘车卡损坏的，到出

（2）Guide passengers with soft ticket and other certificates to exit through manual passageway.

（3）Guide passengers without ticket or incorrect ticket to process at the ticket compensation office.

4. Clear up

（1）Examine automatic check-out machine, manual passageway after all passengers exit and prepare for next check-out.

（2）Guide passengers in the tunnel passageway exit.

（3）Close the gate at the exit after when the work of the day completes.

Key Point 2: Check out under Special Circumstances

1. Deal with Abnormal Situations in Passage Gate

（1）Help passengers pass through the gate in case of incorrect use of the gate.

（2）Check discount certificate of passengers with discount ticket.

（3）Help passengers pass through other gate in case of ticket stuck.

（4）In case of automatic check machine failure, guide passenger pass through other gates or manual passage gates; in case of failure of all automatic machines, check out manually.

2. Ticket Compensation on Passengers' Arrival

（1）Deal with damaged ticket card in

图 6-2 出站检票闸机
Figure 6-2 Check out Gate Machine

口处卡务服务点处理。

（2）对无票、减价不符、乘车卡丢失或无进站记录的旅客，按正常规定补票。

（3）按照旅客应补车次票种正确补票，核对票款，为旅客做好铁路规章及其他相关规定的解释工作。

（4）严格执行票据、现金管理制度，做到票据、现金"入柜加锁、离柜落锁"。

the service office at the exit.

(2) Compensate for passengers without ticket, incorrect discount information, loss of ticket card or entering information.

(3) Compensate correctly for passengers and check the fare, explain regulations and rules patiently to the passengers.

(4) Follow receipt and cash management system strictly, put the receipt and cash in the cabinet with lock.

学习笔记
Study Notes

模块三　课堂练习

分小组模拟出站检票作业（教师可设置检票异常问题）。

Module 3　In-class Exercises

Simulate check-out service in groups (teachers can set some abnormal situations).

模块四　课后拓展

高速铁路乘客出站时，客运员应当检查哪些设备，以确保乘客出站安全？

Module 4　After-class Activity

Which equipment shall be check by the passenger service employees to ensure safe check out?

After-class Activity

任务二 违章乘车的处理

Task 2　Processing of Illegal Boarding

模块一　学前准备

Module 1　Preparation before Class

哪些情况属于违章乘车?

What are the illegal boarding behaviors?

课前学习笔记
Study Notes before Class

模块二　课堂学习

违章乘车包括不符合乘车条件的乘车和车票未按规定办理签证、剪口的乘车。

知识点一：不符合乘车条件的处理

不符合乘车条件的情况是多方面的，由于具体情况不同，处理方法也不同，但归纳起来，可分为两种类型。对不符合乘车条件的旅客、人员，车站应了解原因，区别不同情况予以处理。

（1）属于客观原因，不符合乘车条件的，补收车票票价或票价差额，核收手续费。应买票而未买票的儿童（身高为1.2~1.5米）、身高超过1.5米持用儿童票乘车的儿童，按客观原因处理。

Module 2　In-class Exercises

Illegal boarding behaviors include unconditional boarding, boarding without notes, or with in-punched ticket.

Key Point 1: Handling of Unconditional Boarding

There are many unconditional boarding case and the way to process varies. In general, there are two types. It is required to deal with unconditional passengers or other people accordingly after knowing the reasons. It is required to deal with the situations accordingly.

（1）Unconditional boarding due to objective reasons, fare or fare balance shall be compensated with service charge. Cases such as children（height 1.2~1.5 m）without tickets, and children height more than 1.5 m boarding with child's ticket are dealt with according to objective reasons.

图 6-3　身高购票示意图

Figure 6-3　Ticket Buying Height Introduction

铁路、水路：以身高为分界线，每一名成人旅客可免费携带一名身高不足 1.2 米的儿童；

随同成人旅行的身高 1.2~1.5 米的儿童，应当购买儿童票；

超过 1.5 米时应买全价票。

（2）属于主观原因，即有意取巧、不符合乘车条件的，除按规定补收票价（或票价差额）、核收手续费外，还必须加收应补票价 50% 的票款。具体包括：

① 无票乘车时，补收自乘车站（不能判明时自列车始发站）起至到站止的车票票价。持失效车票乘车按无票处理。

② 持伪造或涂改的车票乘车时，除按无票处理外并送交公安部门处理。

③ 持站台票上车并在车内未补票的，按无票处理。

知识点二：车票未签证、未剪口的处理

（1）旅客未按票面指定的日期、车次乘车（即提前乘车或错过乘车 2 小时以内的），若票价相同的列车时，应补剪、补签，并核收手续费。已使用至到站的车票不再补签；错过乘车超过 2 小时的，车票按失效处理。

divided by height in railway and water transportation: each adult passenger can take a child lower than 1.2m for free;

child with height 1.2~1.5m traveling with adult shall by child's ticket;

child higher than 1.5m shall buy full ticket.

（2）Unconditional boarding with subjective reasons shall compensate the balance fare, service fee, and pay for 50% of the ticket fare additionally. Including:

① Boarding without ticket, compensate from the boarding station (counted from the initial station when the situation is not clear) to the destination station. Boarding with invalid ticket is treated like boarding without ticket.

② Boarding with counterfeited or revised ticket is treated as boarding without ticket and will be handled by policemen.

③ Boarding with platform ticket without compensating in the train is treated as boarding without ticket.

Key Point 2: Dealing with In-noted or In-punched Ticket

（1）Passengers boarding not according to the date, train number on the ticket(boarding in advance, delayed boarding within 2 hours), in case the ticket fare is the same, the ticket shall be punched and noted with service fee. Ticket used to the destination is not noted; delayed boarding beyond 2 hours, the ticket is invalid.

图 6-4 违章乘车
Figure 6-4　Illegal Boarding

（2）买短乘长。

（3）旅客所持车票日期、车次相符但未经车站剪口的应补剪；持通票的旅客中转换乘应签证而未签证的，应补签。补剪、补签，应核收手续费，但已使用至到站的车票不再补剪、补签。

知识点三：违章使用乘车证的处理

（1）违章使用乘车证，如：在票面上加添、涂改、转借、超过有效期限或有效区间乘车未持规定的有关证明、证件或持伪造证明、证件的均按无票处理，要查扣其乘车证及有效证件。此外，单位还应追究其行政责任。对持用伪造乘车证者，一经发现，应立即查扣，并移交公安机关依法处理。超出规定条件使用乘车证者，也按违章使用处理。

（2）Board with short-distance ticket but travel a farther distance.

（3）Passengers boarding with in-pinched ticket of right date and train number shall be punched; passenger with through ticket not noted in transfer station shall be noted. Service fee will be charged. The ticket used to the destination will not be punched or noted.

Key Point 3: Dealing with Illegal Use of Boarding Certificate

（1）Illegal use of boarding certificate, such as adding, revision, lending and borrowing, expiring ticket, or boarding without valid certificate, counterfeited certificate, is treated as boarding without ticket. Boarding certificate pr valid certificated will be confiscated. In addition, administrative liabilities will be accounted. Passengers boarding with counterfeited certificated will be handed over to policemen with certificate confiscated. Passengers boarding without proper

（2）违章使用乘车证均要按所乘旅客列车的等级、席别、铺别、区间（单程或往返）及票面填写人数加倍补收票款，下列乘车证还应按票面记载的席别、区间，按照下列计算方法加收罚款：

① 定期通勤乘车证，按票面填写乘车区间，自有效月份起至发现违章月份止按每月1次往返的里程计算。

② 全年定期乘车证、临时定期乘车证、通勤（学）乘车证。从有效日期（过期的从有效期终了的次日）至发现违章日期止，票面填写的乘车区间在一个铁路局以内的，按每日乘车50千米计算票价；乘车区间跨铁路局的，按每日乘车100千米计算票价，计算后低于50元的按50元核收。

③ 发现其他违章行为的，均按《铁路旅客运输规程》的规定做相应处理。

use of certificate will also be treated as illegal boarding.

（2）Double ticket fare will be charged for illegal use of boarding certificated according to the class, seat and berth class, section (single way or round-way), number of passengers noted on the ticket. The following boarding certificate shall note seat class and section. Double fine is charged according to the following rules:

① Regular communing boarding certificate, travel range is written on the ticket; traveling distance is calculated once a month from the valid month to the month the violation is discovered.

② Annual regular boarding certificate, temporary regular boarding certificate, communing (student) boarding certificate. Ticket fare is calculated by 50 km a day in case the travel range is within the same railway bureau from the valid date (the second day after the valid date for expiring certificate) to the day the violation is discovered; in case the travel distance covers more than one railway bureau, ticket fare is calculated by 100 km a day, and ticket fare below 50 yuan will be charge by 50 yuan.

③ Other violations shall be dealt with in accordance with "Railway Passenger Transportation Regulations".

学习笔记
Study Notes

模块三 课堂练习

（1）无票乘车如何处理？

（2）越站乘车如何处理？

Module 3　In-class Exercises

（1）How to deal with boarding without ticket?

（2）How to deal with station overtaking?

课堂练习
In-class Exercises

模块四　课后拓展

什么是"无纸乘车"？总结无纸乘车的优势。

Module 4　After-class Activity

What is paper-free train taking? Summarize the advantages.

图 6-5　无纸乘车

Figure 6-5　Paper-free Train Taking

After-class Activity

任务三 违章携带物品的处理

Task 3　Deal with Illegal Luggage

模块一　学前准备

请查阅资料，了解高速铁路旅客运输规程中对旅客携带物品的相关规定。

Module 1　Preparation before Class

Search information to understand regulations on passenger luggage in high speed railway passenger transportation.

课前学习笔记
Study Notes before Class

模块二　课堂学习

知识点一：旅客携带物品合规的判定

1. 旅客可免费携带物品的判定（《铁路旅客运输规程》第五十一条）

Module 2　In-class Exercises

Key Point 1: Luggage Judging Standard

1. Standard of Free Luggage（Article 51 of "Railway Passenger Transportation Regulations"）

图 6-6　行李安检计重

Figure 6-6　Luggage Security Check and Weighing

（1）儿童（含免费儿童）10千克，外交人员35千克，其他旅客20千克。每件物品外部尺寸长、宽、高之和不超过160厘米，杆状物品不超过200厘米，但乘坐动车组列车不超过130厘米；重量不超过20千克。

（2）残疾人旅行时代步的折叠式轮椅可免费携带并不计入上述范围。

2. 旅客可限量携带物品的判定（《铁路旅客运输规程》第五十二条）

（1）气体打火机2个，安全火柴2小盒。

（1）10kg for children （including children free of charge）, 35kg for diplomatic personnel, 20kg for other passengers; sum of the length, width and height of the luggage shall be within 160cm; length of rod-shaped luggage shall be less than 200cm and less than 130 for CHR trains; the weight shall be less than 20kg.

（2）Folded wheelchair for the disabled can be taken for free.

2. Standard for Luggage with Limited Quantity （Article 52 of "Railway Passenger Transportation Regulations"）

（1）2 gas lighter, 2 boxes of safe matches.

（2）不超过20毫升的指甲油、去光剂、染发剂。不超过120毫升的摩丝、发胶、卫生杀虫剂、空气清新剂。

（3）军人、武警、公安人员、民兵、猎人凭法规规定的持枪证明携带的枪支子弹。

（4）初生雏20只。

（5）2017年禁带目录中新添物品。

知识点二：禁止携带物品的处理

1. 下列物品不得带入车内：

（1）禁止携带枪支、子弹类（含主要零部件）。

（2）禁止携带爆炸物品类。

（3）禁止携带管制刀具和可能危及旅客人身安全的菜刀、餐刀、屠宰刀、斧子等利器。

（4）禁止携带易燃、易爆物品。

（5）禁止携带剧毒性、腐蚀性、放射性、传染性、危险性物品。

（6）禁止携带危害列车运行安全或公共卫生的物品。

（7）其他禁止和限制旅客携带物品按照国家法律、行政法规、规章规定办理。

（8）违规携带上述物品的，依照国家法律法规的规定处理。

（2）Nail polish, delusterant, hair dye no more than 20mL, hair mousse and spray, pesticide and hair freshener no more than 120mL.

（3）Guns and bullets carried by serviceman, armed policemen, policemen, militiamen and hunters with valid arms license.

（4）20 new born birds.

（5）Other forbidden objects in the catalog issued in 2017.

Key Point 2: Dealing with Forbidden Objects

1. The Following Objects are Prohibited in the Train:

（1）Guns and bullets (major parts included).

（2）Explosives.

（3）Controlled knives, kitchen knives, table knives, butchering knives, axes and other sharp tools that may endanger other passengers.

（4）Flammable and explosive objects.

（5）Toxic, erosive, radioactive, contagious and dangerous objects.

（6）Objects that may endanger safe running of train or public sanitation.

（7）Other prohibited an limited objects are specified according to national laws, rules and regulations.

（8）Any illegal act of bringing the above-mentioned objects will be dealt with according to national laws and regulations.

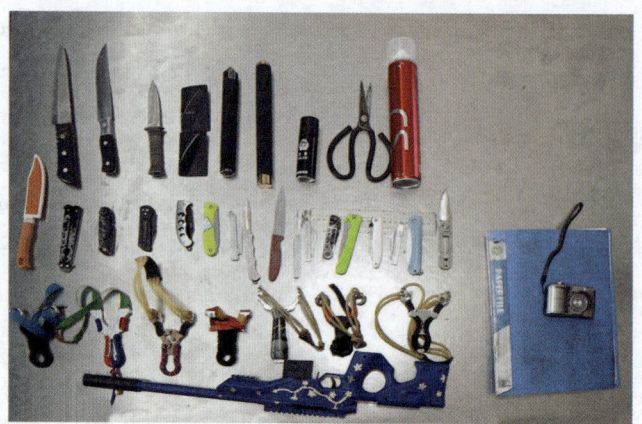

图 6-7　部分违禁物品

Figure 6-7　Some Prohibited Objects

2. 旅客违章携带物品按下列规定处理：

（1）在发站禁止进站上车。

（2）在车内或下车站，对超过免费重量的物品，其超重部分应补收四类包裹运费。对不可分拆的整件超重、超大物品，动物，按该件全部重量补收上车站至下车站四类包裹运费。

2. Passengers' Bringing of Prohibited Objects will be Treated According to the Following Rules:

（1）Prohibited boarding on the departure station.

（2）Over-weight luggage will be charged according to grade 4 luggage in the train or at the destination. Over-weight or over-size luggage that can't be separated or animal shall be charged for the entire item from departure station to the destination.

图 6-8　携带危险物品禁止乘车

Figure 6-8　No Prohibited Objects on the Train

（3）发现危险品或国家禁止、限制运输的物品，妨碍公共卫生的物品，损坏或污染车辆的物品，按该件全部重量加倍补收乘车站至下车站四类包裹运费。危险品交前方停车站处理，必要时移交公安部门处理。对有必要就地销毁的危险品应就地销毁，使之不能为害并不承担任何赔偿责任。没收危险品时，应向被没收人出具书面证明。

（4）如旅客超重、超大的物品价值低于运费时，可按物品价值的50%核收运费。

（5）补收运费时，不得超过本次列车的始发和终点站。

（3）Charge for the dangerous or prohibited objects, unsanitary luggage will be charged from departure station to the destination. Dangerous items shall be handed over at the next station, items endangering or damaging the train shall be charged for with double freight and handed over to the police department. Dangerous items shall be destroyed if necessary. Written certificate shall be issued to its owner on confiscating dangerous objects.

（4）Charge of the 50% of the goods value is feasible in case the transportation fee of the over-weight and over-weight objects is lower than its value.

（5）Charging distance of the transportation fee shall not be longer than the distance from departure station to the destination.

学习笔记
Study Notes

模块三　课堂练习

（1）旅客张某拟于2017年4月25日在北京西站乘坐G307次列车去往重庆北站，由于其腿行动不便（持残疾证）需使用轮椅（可折叠）行动，请问：张某是否可以免费携带轮椅乘车？

（2）旅客陈某于2017年4月10日自石家庄站乘坐G307次列车去往重庆北，且随身携带5瓶密封完好的衡水老白干乘车，请问：该旅客可否将它们携带上车？

Module 3　In-class Exercises

（1）Mr. Zhang took train G307 from Beijing West Railway Station to Chongqing North Station on April 25, 2017, he traveled by a wheelchair (foldable, bringing disability certificate). Could he bring the wheelchair on board for free?

（2）Mr Chen took train G307 from Shijiazhuang Station to Chongqing North Station on April 10, 2017, he brought 5 bottles of sealed Hengshui alcohol, could he bring the bottle on board?

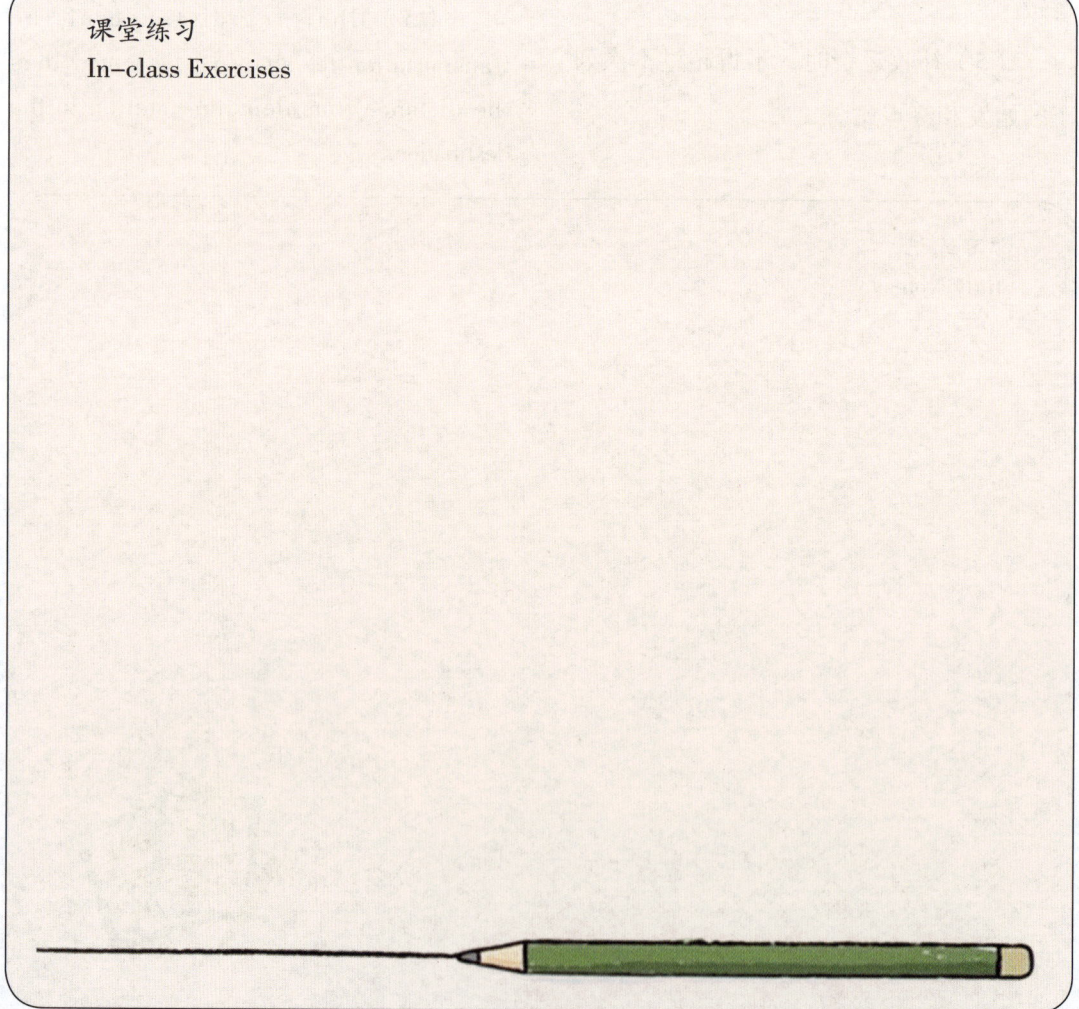

课堂练习
In-class Exercises

模块四　课后拓展

Module 4　After-class Activity

携带超重、超大物品时，运费如何计算？

How to calculate the transportation fee of the over-weigh and over-size luggage?

任务四 车票、证件丢失的处理

Task 4　Dealing with Loss of Ticket or Certificate

模块一　学前准备

Module 1　Preparation before Class

前往当地高铁站或查阅相关网站，了解旅客乘车的新规定。

Learn about the latest rules at the local high speed railway station or on the websites.

课前学习笔记
Study Notes before Class

模块二　课堂学习

知识点一：旅客车票丢失处理

一般在国内的大城市，高铁车票能用身份证验票，其中，进出高铁站都能用身份证，所以，假如有身份证车票验证系统，旅客的票丢了也没关系，可以用身份证出站。如果该站不能用身份证出站，应当挂失补办。具体规定如下：

1. 可办理挂失补的情况

旅客购票后丢失车票时，符合以下条件的，可到车站售票窗口办理挂失补办手续：

（1）提供购票时所使用的有效身份证件原件、原车票乘车日期和购票地车站名称。

（2）不晚于票面发站停止检票时间前20分钟。

Module 2　In-class Learning

Key Point 1: Dealing with Ticket Loss

In large stations of the country, ID card can be used for check-in and check-out, therefore, loss of ticket is no big issue in stations with ID card reading machine. If ID card is not feasible, ticket loss claim and reapplication shall be done. Specific rules are as follows:

1. Cases for Loss Claim and Reapplication

Passengers can claim loss and reapply ticket at the ticket office on meeting the following conditions:

（1）Provide the original ID card used in ticket buying, date of the ticket and station to buy the ticket.

（2）20 minutes ahead of the departure time.

图 6-9　申请挂失补票

Figure 6-9　Ticket Loss Claim and Reapplication

2. 不可办理挂失补的情况

旅客购票后丢失车票，以下情形不办理挂失补办手续：

（1）超过规定时间提出的。

（2）原车票已经退票的。

（3）已经挂失补办的。

3. 挂失补车票的发售、改签和退票的规定

（1）车站确认旅客身份、车票等信息无误后，旅客应按原车票车次、席位、票价重新购买一张新车票。新车票票面标记"挂失补"字样。原车票已经改签的按改签后的车票办理挂失补办手续。

（2）新车票发售后，原车票失效。新车票不能改签，但可以退票；退票时按规定核收补票的手续费。新车票退票后，原车票效力恢复。

（3）旅客持新车票乘车时，应向列车工作人员声明。到站前，列车长确认该席位使用正常的，开具客运记录交旅客作为到站退票的凭证。

（4）旅客到站后24小时内，凭客运记录、新车票和购票时所使用的有效身份证件原件，至退票窗口办理新车票退票手续，按规定核收补票的手续费，不收退票费。

2. Situations Not Suitable for Claim or Reapplication

In the following cases, loss claim or reapplication of ticket is not feasible:

(1) Claim beyond the stipulated time limit.

(2) The ticket being refunded.

(3) The ticket being claimed or reapplied.

3. Selling, Rescheduling and Refunding of Reapplied Ticket

(1) Passenger shall buy a new ticket according to the original train number, seat class and fare after conforming ID. The new ticket is marked with "loss claim and reapplication". Ticket is reapplied according to the rescheduled ticket.

(2) The original ticket is invalid on issuing of the new ticket. The new ticket can't be rescheduled but can be refunded; service fee will be charged on refunding. The original ticket is valid again on refunding of the new ticket.

(3) Passenger shall inform the employee in the train on boarding with new ticket. Head of crew issues passenger transportation certificate for refunding at the destination after confirming the normal use of the seat.

(4) Passenger refunds the new ticket with transportation record, new ticket and valid ID card used for ticket buying within 24 hours after arriving at the destination. Service fee will be charged and there is no refunding fee.

知识点二：挂失补办工作流程

（1）车站指定专门售票窗口办理实名制车票挂失补办手续。旅客办理实名制车票挂失补办手续时，须提供购票时所使用的有效身份证件原件、原车票乘车日期和购票地车站等信息。售票员核实后，须将旅客姓名、有效身份证件名称、号码、原车票乘车日期、车次、车厢、席位和购票地车站等信息登记，经售票主任签字确认后方可办理。挂失新票制出后，登记新票票号。结账时，应对实名制车票挂失补办情况进行审核。

（2）列车接收到站车无线交互系统所提示的车票挂失信息后，对原车票和新车票组织重点查验。持"挂失补"车票的旅客，列车长经确认该席位使用正常的，应开具客运记录，记明旅客姓名、购票时所使用的有效身份证件号码、新车票票号及"席位使用正常，可办理退票"字样。如发现持原车票乘车的旅客时，应按已失效车票处理，按规定补收票款。

Key Point 2: Loss Claim and Reapplication Procedure

（1）Specialized window is set at the station for ticket loss claim and reapplication. Valid ID card in buying ticket, original date and station of buying the ticket is to be provided for reapplication. Ticket seller checks and writes down the information and handle it with the written consent of the ticket selling director. New train number will be noted after making the new ticket. Reapplication information will be checked for reapplied ticket with real name.

（2）The original ticket and new ticket will be checked on receiving ticket loss claim through wireless intercom system. Head of crew shall issue transportation record to passengers with passengers' name, valid ID number in ticket buying, new train number and "normal use of the seat, refund is feasible" after confirming the seat is in normal use. In case the original ticket is used, the original ticket is invalid and fare will be paid again.

客统—1

XX铁路局

客 运 记 录

第18号

记录事由： 移交不明物体击伤旅客

××站：

××年×月×日，××次列车将要运行××站时，运行方向左侧机次第×位第×个车窗外层玻璃被不明物体击碎，将旅客×××，身份证号码××××××××××，持 ××站至××站硬座客快联合票，票号××××××，头部击伤，大约有×公分的口子，血流不止，列车进行了简单包扎处理，该旅客要求下车治疗，现移交你站，请按章处理。

附：旁证材料 2份

注：1、站、车需要编制记录时均适用。

2、本记录不能作为乘车凭证。

站

编制人员 （印）

段

站

签收人员 （印）

段

年 月 日编制

图 6-10 填写客运记录

Figure 6-10 Filling Passenger Transportation Record

（3）对持“挂失补”字样车票和客运记录的旅客，车站出站口的客运服务人员要及时引导至退票窗口办理退票手续。

（4）车站退票窗口，对办理“挂失补”字样车票退票的旅客，须核实客运记录以及“挂失补”字样车票、购票时所使用的有效身份证件原件、旅客一致后，方可理退票，并核收补票的手续费。

（3）Service employee at the exit shall guide passengers with ticket noted with “loss claim and reapplication” and transportation record to refund at the proper window.

（4）Transportation record and, consistence of the valid ID card with the passenger shall be checked for refunding, and service fee will be charged.

学习笔记
Study Notes

模块三　课堂练习

乘车时，有效身份证件丢失如何处理？

Module 3　In-class Exercises

How to deal with the loss of valid ID card during train taking?

课堂练习
In-class Exercises

模块四 课后拓展

讨论：当旅客持挂失补车票越站乘车时应当如何处理？

Module 4　After-class Activity

How to deal with the situation when passenger overtaking the station with reapplied ticket?

任务五 误售、误购、误乘、坐过站的处理

Task 5 Dealing with Mistaken Selling&Buying of Ticket, Mistaking and Missing Stop

模块一 学前准备

请在网上查找误售、误购、误乘的案例。

Module 1 Preparation before Class

Search cases of mistaken selling and buying of tickets, mistaking and missing stop on the Internet.

课前学习笔记
Study Notes before Class

模块二　课堂学习

知识点一：误售、误购处理

（1）发生车票误售、误购时，在发站应换发新票。在中途站、原票到站或列车内应补收票价时，换发代用票，补收票价差额。

应退还票价时，站、车应编制客运记录交予旅客，作为乘车到站要求正当退还票价差额的凭证，并应以最方便的列车将旅客运送至正当到站，均不收取手续费或退票费。

（2）因站名相似或口音不同发生误售、误购时，站、车均应积极主动处理。应补收时，补收正当到站票价与已收票价的差额，收回原票，换发代用票。应退还时，凭原票和客运记录乘车至到站退款。

知识点二：误售、误购、误乘或坐过了站需送回时的处理

（1）因误售、误购或误乘需送回时，承运人应免费将旅客送回。在免费送回区间，旅客不得中途下车。如中途下车，对往返乘车区间补收票价，核收手续费。

（2）旅客因误售、误购、误乘或坐过了站需送回时，列车长应编制客运记

Module 2　In-class Learning

Key Point 1: Dealing with Mistaken Selling and Buying

（1）New ticket shall be issued at the departure station in case of mistaken selling and buying. Substitute ticket is issued at the midway station, original station or fare compensation is required.

In case fare balanced is to be refunded, transportation record shall be written to the passenger at the station and in the train as the certificate for balance refund. Passenger shall be taken to the destination with most convenient train, no service fee or refunding fee is charge.

（2）Mistaken selling or buying occurs due to the similar pronunciation or accent shall be dealt with actively by the station and train employee. Fare balance between the actual and paid price shall be compensated and the original ticket replaced with substitute ticket. Refunding is done at the destination station with the original ticket and passenger transportation record.

Key Point 2: Dealing with Mistaken Selling, Buying, Mistaking the Train and Sending Back Passenger Missing the Stop

（1）In case of sending passengers back due to mistaken selling, buying and missing stop, the carrier shall send passengers back for free. Passenger shall not get off the train in midway during the process. In case the passengers get off midway, ticket fare for the round-way trip shall

录交前方停车站。车站应在车票背面注明"误乘"并加盖站名戳,指定最近列车免费返回。在免费送回区间,站、车均应告知旅客不得自行中途下车。如中途下车,对往返乘车的免费区间,按返程所乘列车等级分别核收往返区间的票价,核收一次手续费。

be charged with service fee.

(2) In case passenger shall be sent back due to mistaken selling or buying of ticket or train stop missing, head of crew shall make passenger transportation record to the next station under the circumstance. The "mistaking" mark shall be made on the back of the ticket with the name of the station and name of the latest train for sending back free of charge. During the process, the passengers shall be informed of the rules of not getting off in midway, or round-way ticket fare and one-time service fee will be charged.

学习笔记
Study Notes

模块三　课堂练习

分小组模拟误售、误购、误乘时的场景。

Module 3　In-class Exercises

Simulate mistaken selling and buying, mistaking the train cases in groups.

课堂练习
In-class Exercises

模块四 课后拓展

误售、误购、误乘应不应该将乘客免费送回起始站？

Module 4　After-class Activity

Shall passengers be sent back to the departure station in case of mistaken selling, buying and mistaking the train?

项目七 高速铁路乘务服务

Project 7　High Speed Railway Passenger Service

任务一　乘务组组成与人员要求

Task 1　Composition and Requirement of Train Attendants

模块一　学前准备

Module 1　Preparation before Class

请你利用网络，查询高铁上有哪些工作人员，并把他们工作中的照片打印粘贴在下方，同时写出对应的岗位名称。

Search the composition of train attendant in high speed railways on the Internet, print the work photos and stick them in the below and write the corresponding post names.

课前学习笔记
Study Notes before Class

模块二　课堂学习

知识点一：乘务组的组成

动车组列车乘务组由客运乘务人员、随车机械师、司机、公安乘警、随车保洁和餐饮服务人员组成，简称"六乘人员"。

Module 2　In-class Learning

Key Point 1: Composition of Train Attendant Crew

CHR train attendant crew consists of train attendants, machinist, driver, railway policemen, train cleaner and catering attendants. And they are called "the six train crew types".

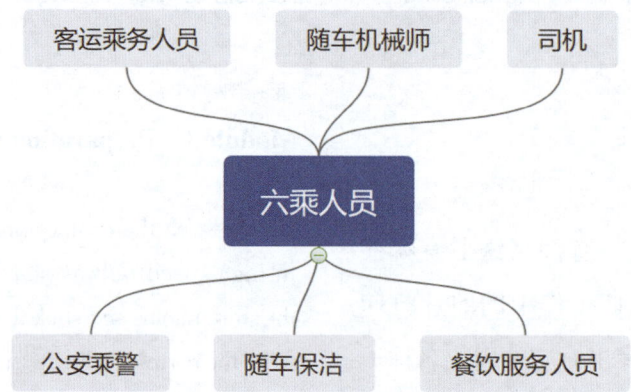

客运乘务人员：train attendants　随车机械师：machinists　司机：driver
公安乘警：railway policemen　随车保洁：train cleaner　餐饮服务人员：catering attendants

图 7-1　动车乘务组"六乘人员"构成

Figure 7-1　Composition of the "Six Train Crew Types" in CHR Train

六乘人员必须在列车长的统一领导下（除行车救援指挥外），分工负责，各司其职，共同做好旅客服务工作。

客运乘务组应采用轮乘制或包乘制，客运乘务组由 1 名列车长和 2 名列车员组成。动车组重联时，按 2 个乘务组安排人员；编组 16 辆的动车组按 1 名列车长和 4 名列车员配备。对运行时间较长的动车组可适当增加客运乘务人员。动

The crew shall work under the leadership of the head of crew (except rescue commander), and they serve the passengers together with performing their own duties.

The crew work on shifting or crew responsible system, and the attendant team consists of 1 head and 2 attendants. In case of CHR train group connection, two teams are arranged; the CHR train with 16 coaches is equipped with team of 1 head and 4 attendants. Number of attendants can be increased for

车组司机实行单司机值乘制，随车机械师按每组1人配备。

trains running for a long period. Single driver shifting system is applicable in CHR trains and 1 machinist is set for each group.

高铁乘务员：train attendant　司机：driver　随车机械师：machinist
高铁乘警：railway policeman　高铁随车保洁：train cleaner　餐饮服务人员：catering attendant

图7-2　高铁动车乘务组"六乘人员"构成
Figure 7-2　Attendant Composition of High Speed Railway Attendant Crew

知识点二：乘务组人员要求

1. 基本要求

（1）客运人员应具备高中及以上文化程度，能够熟练使用计算机、服务设施设备、消防器材，掌握常用英语会话，具有良好的语言文字表达能力和服务技巧，五官端正、身材匀称。女性身高一般不低于1.60米，男性身高一般不低于1.70米。

（2）客运人员应当按照规定进行岗前培训，列车长培训由铁路局（集团公司）负责，列车员培训由客运段负责，经考试合格后，由铁路局（集团公司）统一颁发上岗证，持证上岗。上岗后应按规定进行适应性培训和定期脱产培训。

（3）动车组列车餐饮、随车保洁人员应五官端正、身材匀称，保持队伍相对稳定，遇有人员变动，应当通知列车所属的铁路局客运处。餐饮、保洁人员上岗前应委托站段进行铁路安全知识、应急演练和设备操作培训。培训及考核发证由铁路局负责，持证上岗。上岗时应穿着统一服装、佩戴工号牌。

2. 应具备的品质

（1）具有高度的工作责任心，全心全意为他人服务，忠于职守，热爱乘务工作，具有良好的工作态度。

Key Point 2: Requirements for Train Attendants

1. Basic Requirements

（1）Passenger service employees shall be high school graduates or above, skilled in using computer, service facilities, fire extinguishing equipment, command of English for daily use, ability of expressing and service skill, well-featured and well proportioned. Height of female employee is not lower than 1.60 m and male employee not lower than 1.70 m.

（2）Pre-employment training shall be done according to regulations. Training of head of crew is done by railway bureau (company group) and training of train attendant is done by passenger traffic section. After passing the exams, work license is issued by railway bureau (company group) to work with license. Adaptive training and regular off-job training shall be done during work.

（3）Catering and cleaning service employees in CHR trains shall be well featured and well proportioned. The team shall be relatively fixed; passenger traffic service office shall be informed in case of personnel change. Training of safety knowledge, emergency drill and equipment operation shall be done for catering and cleaning service employees shall be done by traffic sections before work. Railway bureau is responsible for issuance of training and exam certificate, employees should be certified to work. Uniform shall be worn with work number card during work.

2. Qualities Required

（1）High sense of responsibility, serve

（2）遵守国家法令、法规和铁路条例规章，严守国家机密。团结协作，谦虚谨慎，平等待人。爱护公共财物，廉洁奉公，公私分明，管理好列车上的供应品，不贪占企业财物。

（3）努力钻研业务，丰富社会知识，研究旅客心理，探索旅客需求，不断提高服务技能，提高处理突发事件的能力，做好乘务工作。

passengers wholeheartedly, devoted to work with good attitude.

（2）Obey national laws, regulations and railway rules, maintain national secrets. Spirit of teamwork with modesty, treat everyone with equality. Cherish public properties, be public-spirited with integrity. Well management of supplies in the train without embezzlement.

（3）Diligence in work with constant learning of common senses, study of passengers' psychology and requirement to improve service skills and ability to handle with emergencies.

图 7-3　高铁动车乘务组人员出乘

Figure 7-3　CHR Crew on Duty

学习笔记
Study Notes

模块三 课堂练习

（1）请你利用网络查询并写出：什么是"轮乘制"？什么是"包乘制"？你认为两者的不同是什么。

（2）头脑风暴：以小组为单位，讨论并写出：你认为高铁"六乘人员"分别应该具备哪些重要品质，以及理由。讨论结束后，以小组为单位进行分享。

Module 3　In-class Exercises

（1）Search information on the Internet and write down the definiton of, and differences between crew shifting system and responsible crew system.

（2）Brainstorm: discuss in groups and write down the qualities required for the six types of crew teams in high speed railway and the reasons. Share the results with other groups after discussion.

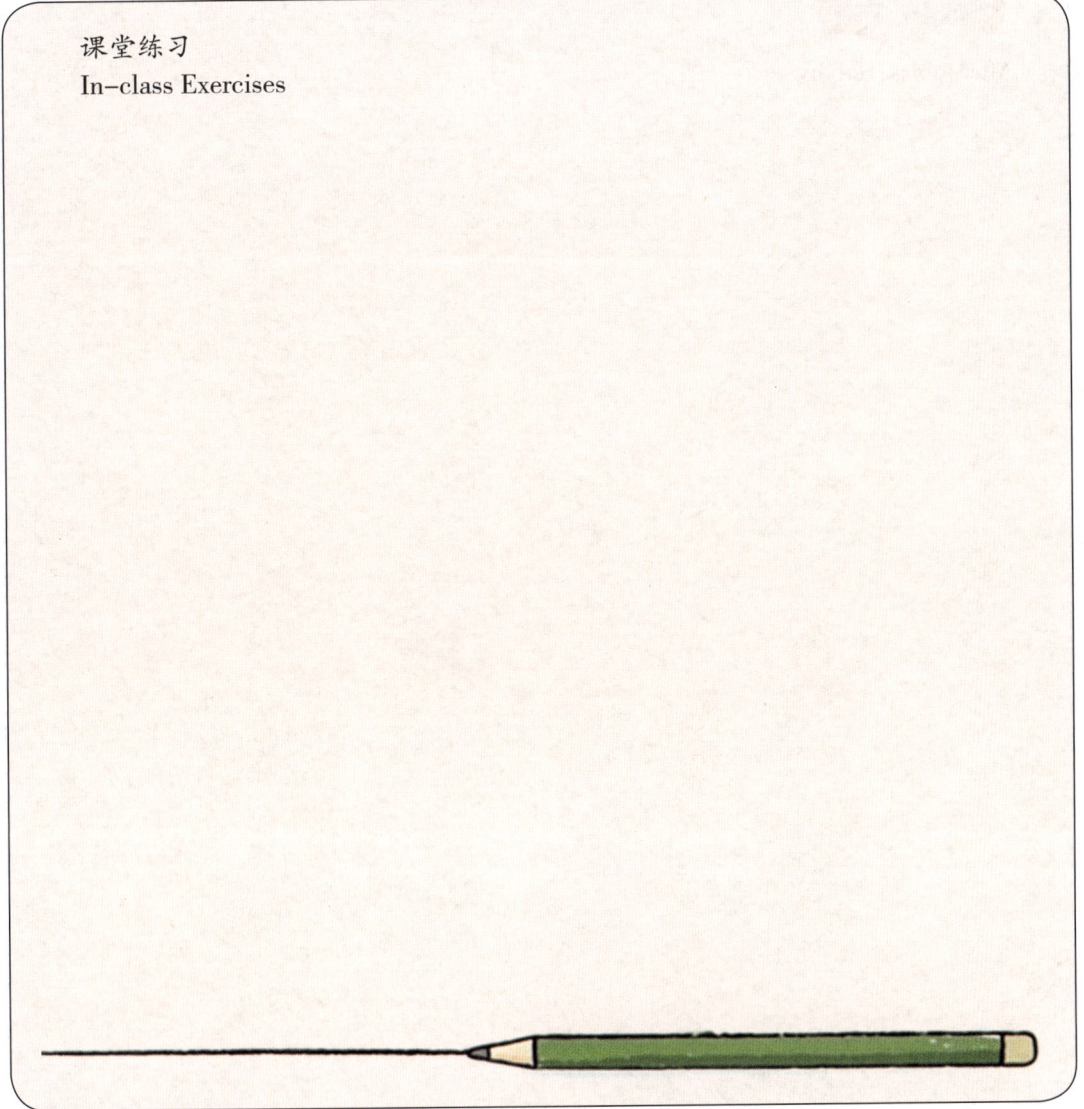

课堂练习
In-class Exercises

模块四　课后拓展

请你利用网络查询目前世界上高铁服务质量较高的三个国家，并将这些国家的高铁工作人员进行服务的照片打印、粘贴在下面，同时配上文字说明：为什么他们的服务做得很好。

Module 4　After-class Activity

Search on the Internet for the information of three countries with high-quality high speed railway service, and print the employees' pictures in work. Write down the reasons for their high-quality service.

课后拓展
After-class Activity

任务二 主要乘务人员岗位职责

Task 2　Job Description of Major Crew Members

模块一　学前准备

Module 1　Preparation before Class

你坐过高铁吗？如果坐过，请你说说高铁上你看到的工作人员分别做了哪些事情。如果没坐过高铁，请你利用网络查询：高铁上的工作人员主要的工作内容是什么？

Have you taken high speed trains? Talk about the job done by the crew if you have. Search information on the Internet about their work if you have not.

课前学习笔记
Study Notes before Class

模块二 课堂学习

知识点一：列车长的职责

（1）执行规章制度，履行岗位职责。服从调度指挥，完成上级布置的各项任务。

（2）负责组织、指挥、协调各工种作业，召开出、退乘会。督促乘务员按照标准作业，确保服务质量及车内安全，完成上级布置的各项任务。

（3）负责监督和检查整备、保洁、餐饮工作。

（4）负责检查动车组列车安全、服务设施设备，发现设备故障，及时反馈给随车机械师处理。

（5）负责与司机、随车机械师等岗位保持作业联控，并与车站办理交接。

（6）负责办理乘务过程中的各项客运业务，收集旅客对列车服务工作的意见，受理旅客投诉，帮助旅客解决困难。

（7）负责动车组列车非正常情况下的应急处置，并及时向派班室（客调）及上级部门汇报。

（8）负责乘务组在折返站停留期间的工作安排和人员管理。

（9）监督乘务员在值乘中各个阶段保持专业化形象。负责乘务组在折返站及住宿期间的管理。

（10）负责各类信息的反馈，并提出改进建议。

Module 2 In-class Learning

Key Point 1: Job Description of Head of Crew

（1）Carry out rules and regulations, perform job responsibilities. Obey dispatching and commanding to complete tasks.

（2）In charge of organizing, commanding and coordinating jobs of all post, call work starting and completion meeting. Urge attendant to work in accordance with standards to ensure the completion of work with standard, safety of the train and fulfill the tasks assigned.

（3）In charge of supervising and examination of preparation, cleaning and catering.

（4）In charge of safety check of trains and service facilities, and informing machinists of necessary repair.

（5）Connected control of driver and machinists, job connecting with stations.

（6）Processing all kinds of passenger transportation service, receiving passengers' complaints and help them with possible trouble.

（7）Emergency disposal of CHR trains and prompt report to the dispatching office and superior departments.

（8）Job arrangement and staff management during stay in the turn-back station.

（9）Supervising professional image of the crew, staff management in the turn-back station and the staying period.

（10）Information feedback and make suggestion.

图 7-4 工作中的高铁列车长
Figure 7-4 CHR Train Head of Crew in Work

知识点二：客运乘务员的职责

（1）在列车长的领导下，完成乘务工作。

（2）负责实施列车服务和车内安全工作。

在车站，确认旅客乘降情况，通知司机或随车机械师关闭动车组车门。

发生危及行车和旅客生命安全的紧急情况时，使用紧急制动阀停车或通知司机采取措施；需要组织旅客撤离列车时，通知司机，由司机向列车调度员报告或通知就近车站值班员；在司机指挥下，处理有关事故救援等事宜。

（3）负责本次列车各种服务备品的检查。

车上移动备品包含饮水机、微波炉、

Key Point 2：Job Description of Passenger Service Employee

（1）Finish work under the leadership of hand of crew.

（2）Ensure passenger service and safety in the train.

Confirming passenger elevating status in the station, inform driver or machinist of door closing.

In case of emergency that may endanger the safety of train and passengers, stop the train with emergency stop valve or inform the driver; inform the driver if passenger evacuation is necessary, and the driver reports it to the dispatcher or person on duty in the nearest station; process rescue under the commanding of the driver.

（3）Check of service facilities in the train.

Mobile equipment in the train are

移动座椅、安全锤（含盒）以及应急乘降梯、车门安全带等设备。

（4）协助做好本次列车的配餐工作。

（5）负责完成规定的广播任务。

（6）负责实施车内各类紧急情况的处置。

（7）完成规定的作业流程，并达到质量标准。

（8）负责向列车长反映各种信息，提出合理化建议。

（9）完成列车长交办的其他工作。

drinking machine, microwave oven, mobile seat, safety hammer (box included), emergency lift, door safety belt and so on.

(4) Help with catering in the train.

(5) Broadcast as required.

(6) Handling emergencies.

(7) Finish required work with quality.

(8) Report to the head of crew and make reasonable suggestion.

(9) Finish other work required by head of crew.

图 7-5 工作中的高铁客运乘务员

Figure 7-5 High Speed Train Attendant in Work

知识点三：动车组司机的职责

（1）执行规章制度，服从调度指挥，履行岗位职责。

（2）在区间非正常停车时，负责指挥处理有关行车、列车防护和事故救援

Key Point 3: Job Description of CHR Train Driver

(1) Carry out rules and regulations, obey dispatching and commanding to perform job duties.

(2) In case of irregular stop between

等工作；在其他非正常情况下，协助列车长实施应急预案。

（3）出动车所后，负责有关型号动车组的车门集控开关，在车站，列车在规定位置停稳后开启车门；开车前，根据客运列车长通知，关闭车门。

（4）动车组列车发生故障时，按车载信息监控装置的提示，按步骤及时处理；需要由随车机械师配合处理时，与随车机械师共同处理。需调车作业或救援时，配合随车机械师安装过渡车钩，并实施相关联挂作业。

（5）负责与调度日常联络，接受传达上级命令指示。

（6）执行动车组回送任务。

stations, in charge of train running, protection and accident rescue; help head of crew with performing emergency plan in other irregular cases.

（3）Centralized control of doors of various types of CHR trains after leaving train parking lot; open the door after stable stop at the station; closed the door on the notice of head of crew before departure.

（4）Instant process of train default under the instruction of the information supervision device in the train; cooperate with machinists if necessary. Cooperate with machinist to install transitional train coupler if train dispatching for rescue is needed and finish coupling.

（5）In charge of regular connection with dispatcher, receiving and transmitting orders from superiors.

（6）In charge of CHR trains sending back.

图 7-6 工作中的动车组司机

Figure 7-6　CHR Train Driver in Work

学习笔记
Study Notes

模块三 课堂练习

（1）头脑风暴：以小组为单位，分别总结出高铁列车长、乘务员、司机的主要岗位职责是什么。同时组内进行头脑风暴，讨论并写出你们组认为每个岗位最重要的岗位职责分别是什么，并给出你们组的理由。

（2）角色扮演互动：每组派出1位同学随机扮演高铁乘务组工作人员，并通过自己的动作及服务语言给其他组同学提示，其他组同学进行抢答，猜测他扮演的是高铁乘务组中的哪一个岗位。猜中的小组加5分，猜错的小组扣5分。各个小组轮流上台扮演，最终积分最高的小组则为胜利。（注意：在每组进行完角色扮演后，教师应对角色扮演的同学的表现进行点评。）

Module 3 In-class Exercises

（1）Brainstorm：work in groups to summarize the job responsibilities of head of crew, train attendants and driver. Discuss and write down the most important work of each post, and your reasons.

（2）Role play: one student in each group plays a crew member in high speed train, student in other groups guess the specific post through action and language. The groups take turns in role play. The winning group shall win 5 points and losing group lose 5 points and the group with highest pints win. (Notice: Teacher shall comment the presentation of each group.)

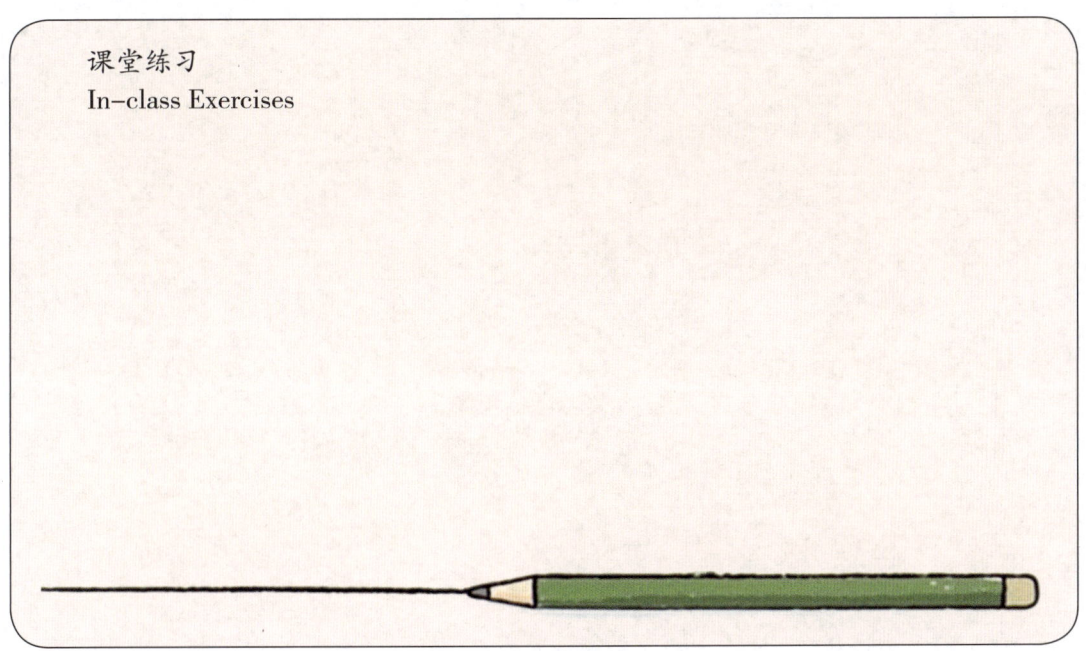

课堂练习
In-class Exercises

模块四　课后拓展

请你利用网络查询：高速铁路乘务组中，除了列车长、乘务员、司机，还有哪些工作人员？他们的主要工作职责是什么？请你写下来。

Module 4　After-class Activity

Search on the Internet: what are the other crew members except head of crew, train attendant and drive? Write down their major duties?

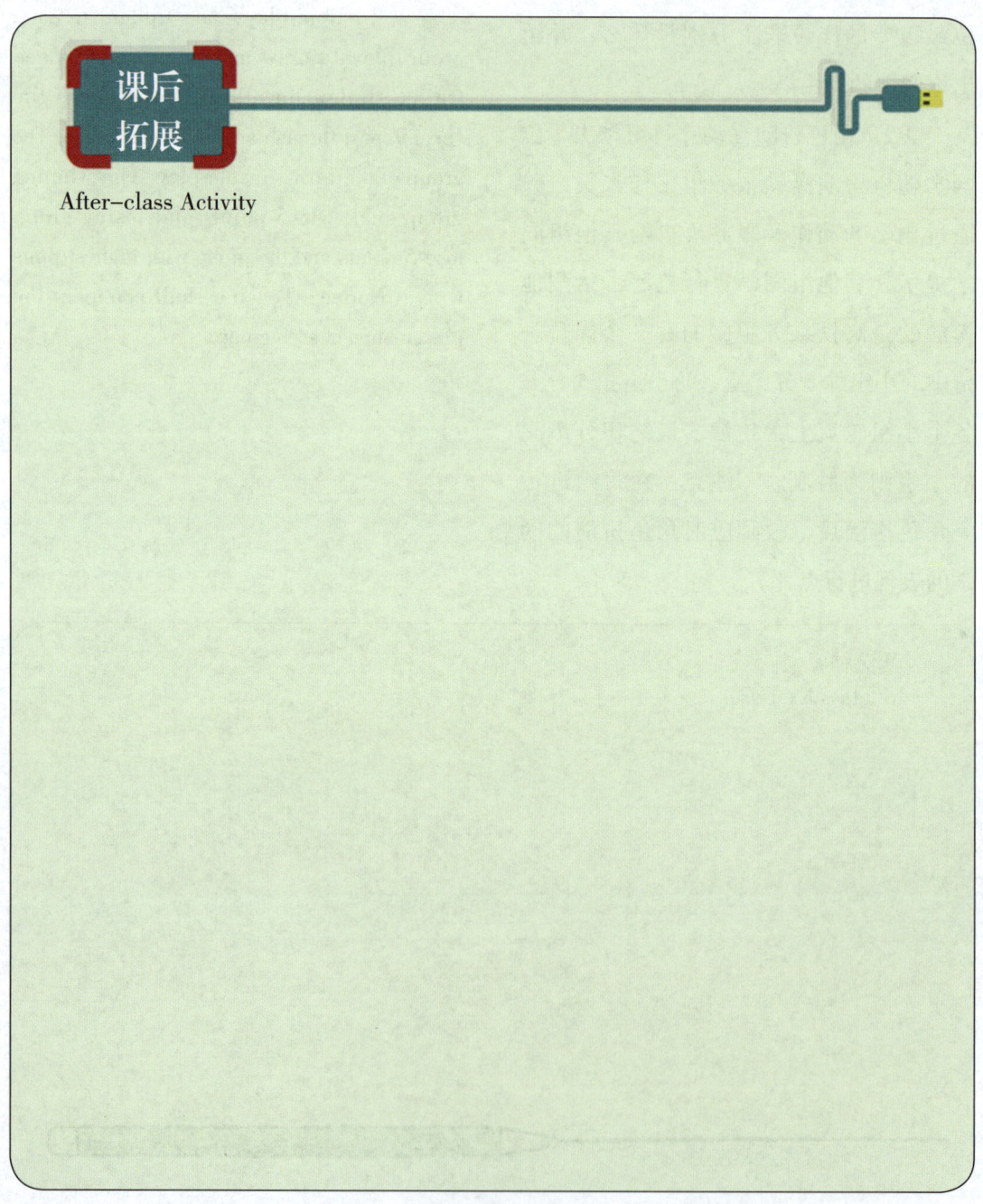

任务三　乘务工作服务流程

Task 3　Passenger Service Procedure

模块一　学前准备

Module 1　Preparation before Class

你坐过高铁吗？如果坐过，请你回想并整理：从你候车到下车的整个过程中，列车上的乘务工作人员依次做了哪些事情？如果你还没坐过高铁，请你试着利用网络寻找上述问题的答案，并整理好写下来。

Have you taken high speed train? Recall the process from waiting to check out, what are the jobs done by the service employee in the train if you have. Search answer to the above question on the Internet if you have not, and write it down.

课前学习笔记
Study Notes before Class

模块二　课堂学习

知识点一：准备阶段

1. 列车长准备

（1）到派班室报到或电话联系，接受命令指示，确认当日担当乘务情况，填写乘务报告，按时出乘。出乘前命令指示记录准确、无遗漏，乘务任务明确。

（2）检查通信设备、乘务资料等携带情况。乘务资料包括电报、客运记录、票务处理必要的资料。

（3）列车开车前40分钟在站台接车，召开出乘会，检查乘务员仪容仪表、着装、应配物品，布置乘务任务。

（4）全面巡视车用，检查车内保洁、备品和饮用水配置情况，督促保洁人员补做车内卫生，并做好交接记录。

（5）与司机、随车机械师对表，联系有关事宜，清楚了解设备状况。

2. 列车员准备

（1）整理仪容仪表，检查对讲机等设备、资料携带情况。

（2）列车开车前40分钟在站台接车，参加出乘会，接受列车长的命令指示。

（3）全面巡视车厢，检查车内保洁和备品配置情况，督促保洁人员补做车内卫生。

Module 2　In-class Exercises

Key Point 1：Preparation

1. Preparation of Head of Crew

（1）Go to the dispatching room and call the room for order to confirm the service status of the day and fill in the report. Start work on time. Ensure accurate and complete order record and specific duty tasks.

（2）Check communication equipment, and document. Passenger service document include telegraph, passenger transportation record and necessary files for ticket handling.

（3）Receiving at the platform 40 minutes before departure, call service meeting, check appearance, dress and allocated devices of the crew, and assign the work.

（4）Full check of supplies of the train, examine deployment of cleaning, spare parts and drinking water in the train; urge cleaners of cleaning in the train record the handover statues.

（5）Set watch with diver and machinist for connection, get a clear knowledge of the equipment.

2. Preparation of Train Attendant

（1）Check appearance and dress, check walkie-talkie and documents.

（2）Receive the train at the platform 40 minute before departure, attending the starting meeting to receive orders from the head of crew.

（3）Full check supplies of the train, examine deployment of cleaning, spare parts and drinking water in the train; urge cleaners of cleaning in the train record the handover statues.

图 7-7 高铁乘务员巡视列车，做好准备
Figure 7-7 Attendant Checking the Train and Getting Prepared

知识点二：乘务阶段

1. 开车前

（1）列车长。

① 在指定位置立岗。列车长在随车机械师值乘位置附近为宜，与车站客运值班员办理交接，掌握售票情况。

② 检查餐饮供应准备情况。

③ 引导重点旅客。做好开车前 5 分钟广播通告。做到引导有序，妥善安排，通告及时。与乘务员联系，确认旅客乘降完毕，通知司机关闭车门。

（2）列车员。

在与列车长所在位置相对应的列车另一端，引导旅客。做到引导有序，妥善安排重点旅客。确认旅客乘降完毕，报告列车长。

Key Point 2: Passenger Service Period

1. Before Departure

（1）Head of crew.

① Stand at the designated position. Head of crew stand near the machinist, hand over with passenger service employee at the station to get the knowledge of the ticket selling.

② Check catering service preparation.

③ Guide special passengers. Broadcast 5 minutes before departure for orderly guidance, proper arrangement and instant notice. Contact with train attendant to confirm boarding status and inform the driver to close the doors.

（2）Train attendant.

Standing ant the other end of train parallel to the head of crew to guide passenger. Orderly guidance and care for special passengers. Report to the head of crew after confirming completion of boarding.

图 7-8 高铁乘务员引导旅客
Figure 7-8 Attendant Guiding Passengers

2. 开车后

（1）列车长。

① 在 10 分钟之内播完欢迎词及相关内容（通报站名、服务设施介绍、安全提示等），随后可播放背景音乐。

② 巡视车厢，查验车票，检查行李摆放情况，提醒旅客将大件行李及铁器、锐器等不适宜放在行李架上的物品放在指定位置并自行看管。

（2）列车员。

① 巡视车厢，检查行李摆放情况，提醒旅客将大件行李及铁器、锐器等不适宜放在行李架上的物品放在指定位置并自行看管。

② 协助列车长查验车票。

2. After Departure

（1）Head of crew.

① Finish broadcasting welcome speech and relative content（station announcement, service facilities, safety instruction）, and play background information.

② Tour coaches and check tickets, luggage status, remind passengers to put large luggage, iron and sharp item on the designated place and take care by themselves.

（2）Train attendant.

① Tour coaches and check tickets, luggage status, remind passengers to put large luggage, iron and sharp item on the designated place and take care by themselves.

② Assist head of crew with ticket checking.

图 7-9 高铁列车长和乘务员查验车票

Figure 7-9 High Speed Train Head of Crew and Attendant Checking Ticket

3. 运行中

（1）列车长。

① 巡视车厢，掌握车内动态，处理服务过程中的各类问题。做到重点旅客心中有数，主动提供帮助。特殊情况要妥善处理，汇报准确及时。

② 检查途中保洁作业质量。

③ 做好开车后和到站前广播通告，遇有列车晚点超过 15 分钟时，通过广播向旅客致歉。组织中途停站旅客乘降。

④ 途中停站，与车站客运值班员办理交接。

（2）列车员。

① 巡视车厢，掌握车内动态，处理服务过程中的各类问题。耐心解答旅客问询，做好解释工作。对重点旅客心中有数，主动提供帮助。特殊情况妥善处理。

3. Train Running

（1）Head of crew.

① Tour coaches to know the status in the train. Handle possible problems, care and help for special passengers. Proper handling of unexpected situations with accurate and instant report.

② Check cleaning status in the train.

③ Broadcasting before departure and arrival. In case the train is delayed for over 15 minutes, broadcast for apology. Organizing boarding and getting off in intermediate stops.

④ Hand over with employee on duty in stops.

（2）Train attendant.

① Tour coaches to know the status in the train. Handle possible problems, answer passengers' questions with patience. Handle possible problems, care and help for special passengers. Proper handling of unexpected situations.

图 7-10 高铁乘务员耐心解答旅客问询
Figure 7-10 Attendant Answering Passengers' Questions

② 做好车厢内卫生清洁,保证干净整洁,卫生达标。

③ 协助列车长做好到站前 5 分钟广播通报站名、到开时刻;提醒旅客做好在列车运行前方车门下车准备。开车后 5 分钟内广播预告前方停车站及相关内容(通报站名、服务设施介绍、安全提示等)。

4. 终到前后

(1) 列车长。

① 征求旅客意见建议。做到态度诚恳,记录详细。

② 到站前 5 分钟广播通报站名,致道别词,提醒旅客做好下车准备,请旅客配合尽快下车。

③ 列车到站后,向旅客道别,协助重点旅客下车。

④ 旅客下车完毕,从大号车厢开始

② Clean the coaches to meet sanitation standard.

③ Help head of crew with broadcast of name of stops, time of arrival and departure 5 minutes before arrival; remind passengers to get off in the front door of the coach. Broadcast next station and other relevant information (name of stop, service facilities, safety instruction) within 5 minutes of departure.

4. Before Arriving Destination

(1) Head of crew.

① Ask for passengers' advice sincerely and write them down in details.

② Broadcast name of stop 5 minutes before arrival, deliver farewell speech; remind passengers to get ready for arrival as soon as possible.

③ Farewell to passengers and help special passengers to get off.

④ Tour the coaches for possible missing items from the one with big numbers after all passengers getting off.

巡视，检查有无旅客遗失物品等。

⑤ 在规定位置与车站客运值班员办理重点旅客、遗失物品等业务交接。

（2）列车员。

① 协助列车长做好到站前5分钟广播通报站名，致道别词，提醒旅客做好下车准备，请旅客配合尽快下车。

② 列车到站后，向旅客道别，协助重点旅客下车。做到用语规范，微笑致意。

③ 旅客下车完毕，从小号车厢开始，检查有无旅客遗失物品等，发现问题报告列车长。

⑤ Hand over special passengers and lost objects with employee on the station at the designated position.

(2) Train attendant.

① Help head of crew with Broadcast name of stop 5 minutes before arrival, deliver farewell speech; remind passengers to get ready for arrival as soon as possible.

② Farewell to passengers and help special passengers to get off with standard language and smile.

③ Tour the coaches for possible missing items from the one with small numbers after all passengers getting off. Report possible problems to head of crew.

图 7-11 旅客下车完毕，高铁乘务员巡视列车

Figure 7-11 Attendant Touring Coaches

知识点三：退乘阶段

1. 列车长

（1）召开退乘会，讲评当日工作，填写乘务报告。

（2）对随车保洁情况作出鉴定。

（3）带领乘务组退乘。

（4）需要解款时到规定地点缴款。

2. 列车员

（1）参加退乘会，汇报当日乘务工作情况。

（2）协助列车长到指定地点缴款。

Key Point 3: Leaving Post

1. Head of Crew

（1）Call for meeting and comment on the work of the day, fill in service report.

（2）Evaluate cleaning status.

（3）Lead the crew to leave the post.

（4）In case of money transfer, hand in the money at the designated place.

2. Train Attendant

（1）Attend the meeting and report the service status of the day.

（2）Help head of crew with money handing in at the designated place.

图 7-12 高铁乘务员列队退乘

Figure 7-12　Attendants Leaving the Post in a Queue

学习笔记

Study Notes

模块三　课堂练习

以小组为单位，对高铁乘务工作服务流程进行模拟演练。演练前，每组从"准备阶段、乘务阶段、退乘阶段"中分别抽取一个需要展示的内容。抽完展示的内容后，进行30分钟的情节设计及排练（设计的动作及台词写在下框），力求将抽取的内容较为全面地展示出来。分组展示结束后，老师进行点评。

Module 3　In-class Exercises

Simulate service process in groups. Each group select one procedure among "preparation stage" "service stage" and "leaving post stage" before simulation. Each group has 30 minutes for preparation and rehearsal before presentation （write down the gestures and lines in the box below） and try to present the content completely. The teacher comment after each presentation.

课堂练习
In-class Exercises

模块四　课后拓展

请你查询网络资料：目前在高铁上，乘客最常询问乘务员的问题有哪些？乘务员的对应回答是什么？请你整理并写下来。

Module 4　After-class Activity

Search on the Internet and write down the most frequently asked questions by the passengers in high speed trains? And what are the answers. Collect them and write them down.

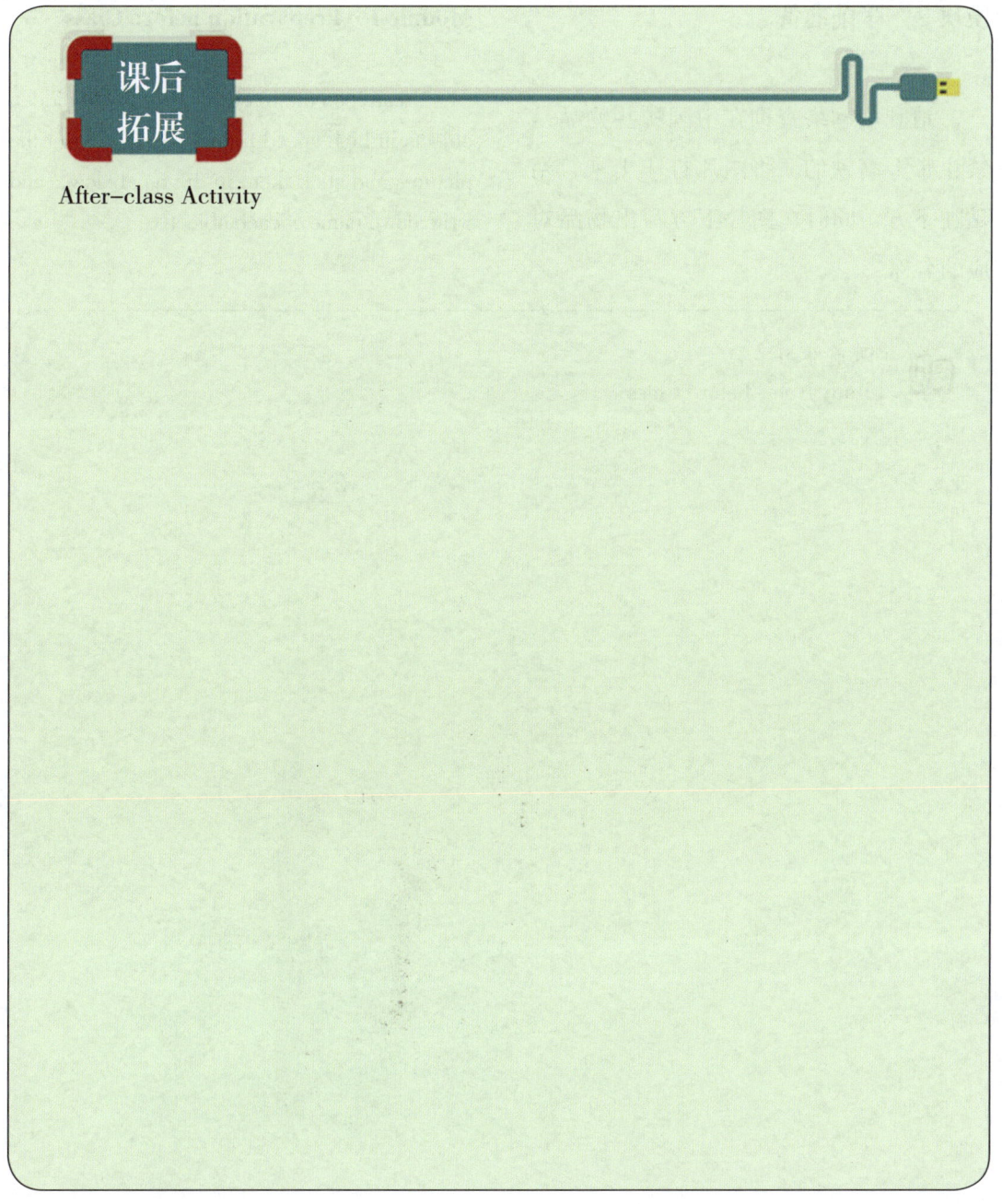
After-class Activity

任务四 动车组突发情况处理

Task 4 Emergency Handling in CHR Trains

模块一 学前准备

请利用网络查询在中国哪些物品是禁止带上高铁的。将图片打印出来，粘贴在下方，同时在图片下方写出物品对应的名称。

Module 1 Preparation before Class

Search on the Internet about the forbidden objects in high speed trains in China. Print the pictures and stick them in the box below, and write down name of each object.

课前学习笔记
Study Notes before Class

模块二 课堂学习

知识点一：旅客因病下车的处理

（1）发生旅客伤病时，提供协助。通过广播寻求医护人员帮助，情形严重的，报告客运调度。

（2）发现行为、神情异常旅客时，重点关注，配备乘警的列车通知乘警到场处理；未配备乘警的列车由列车长处理，情形严重时交列车运行前方停车站处理。

（3）对无同行人监管的行为、神情异常旅客，列车长可采取必要的看护措施，情形严重时交列车运行前方停车站处理；有同行人时应介绍安全注意事项，并予以协助。

Module 2　In-class Learning

Key Point 1：Passenger Getting off Due to Illness

（1）Help passengers with illness and injuries. Broadcast for medical help. Report it to dispatching center for serious situation.

（2）Special care for passengers with abnormal behaviors or expression, inform train police; inform the head of crew in trains without train police; hand it over to the next stop in serious emergency.

（3）Head of crew shall pay special care for passengers without custody those with abnormal behaviors or expression; or hand it over to the next station in serious situations; introduce safety instructions to their travel partner and provide necessary help.

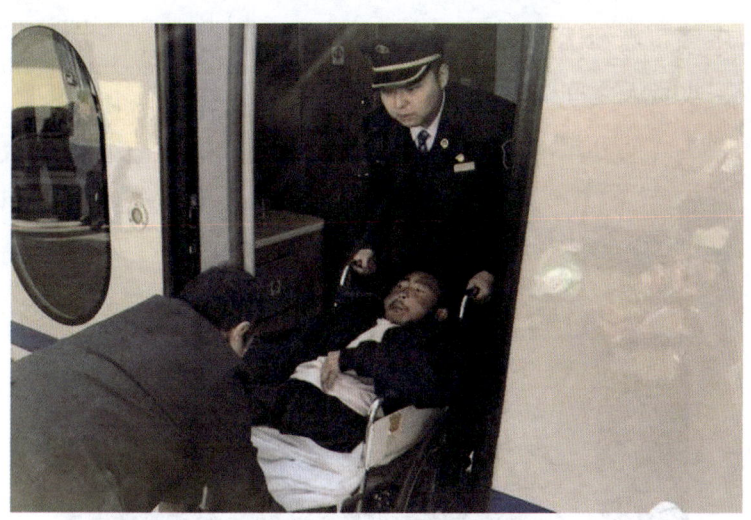

图 7-13　高铁旅客因病下车

Figure 7-13　Ill Passengers Getting off the Train

知识点二：旅客无票乘车拒绝补票的处理

（1）发现无票乘车并拒绝补票的旅客，列车长可责令其下车并应编制客运记录交县、市所在地车站或三等以上车站处理（其到站近于上述到站时，应交到站处理）。

（2）列车移交的上述人员应在移交站按规定进行补票。除缴纳手续费外，还应缴纳应补票价50%的票款。

（3）对列车上拒绝补票的人，应编制客运记录交列车前方县、市三等以上车站处理，但不能超过无票人员的到站。车站对列车移交和本站发现的人员应按章补票价，对当时无力补交者，应设法通过其单位或家属帮助补交票款。

（4）客运记录：指在旅客或行李、包裹运输过程中因特殊情况，承运人与旅客、托运人、收货人之间需记载某种事项或车站与列车之间办理业务交接的文字凭证。

Key Point 2: Handling with Passengers Boarding without Ticket Rejection Compensation

(1) Head of crew shall ask the passenger to get off and compile passenger transportation record to station at the county or municipal level or grade 3 station or above (in case the passengers' destination is nearer than the stations, hand it to the destination station).

(2) The above-mentioned passengers shall compensate at the transferred station, service fee and and additional payment of 50% of ticket fare shall be paid.

(3) Passenger transportation record for compensation rejection shall be made to hand it to the grade 3 county and municipal stations, and the station shall not exceed the passengers' destination. The station shall ask the passengers for compensation, for passengers incapable of compensating, inform his institution or family member for compensation.

(4) Passenger transportation record: it is the written receipt recording the service between carrier and passengers, consignor and receiver or stations in special cases during passenger, luggage or package transportation.

图 7-14　高铁列车长及乘务员查验车票

Figure 7-14　Head of Crew and Train Attendant Checking Ticket

知识点三：列车上发现危险物品的处理

（1）发现危险物品或国家禁止、限制运输的物品，妨碍公共卫生的物品，损坏或污染车辆的物品，按该件全部重量加倍补收乘车站至下车站四类包裹运费。危险物品交前方停车站处理，必要时移交公安部门处理。对有必要就地销毁的危险物品应就地销毁，使之不能危害并不承担任何赔偿责任。没收危险品时，应向被没收人出具书面证明。

Key Point 3: Handling Dangerous Objects in Train

（1）Transportation expenses for type 4 package shall be double charged from departure station to destination for dangerous, forbidden, limited transportation objects or objects that may affect public health, damage or pollute the train. Dangerous objects shall be handed to the next station, or to the police department if necessary. Dangerous objects shall be destroyed to eliminate the hazard if necessary without assuming liability for damage. Written certificate shall be issued to the owner when confiscating the dangerous objects.

图 7-15 铁路警方在高铁安检口查获危险物品

Figure 7-15 Railway Police Discovering Dangerous Object at the Safety Check Entrance

（2）发现旅客携带品可疑及无人认领的物品时，配备乘警的列车通知乘警到场处理；未配备乘警的列车由列车长处理，对危险品做好登记、保管及现场处置，并交前方停车站（公安部门）处理。

（2）Train police shall deal with suspicious unclaimed objects; head of crew shall deal with the situation in trains without policemen to record, store and handle with them, and hand it to the next station (police department).

知识点四：物品遗失的处理

（1）《中华人民共和国铁路旅客运输规程》规定：对旅客的遗失物品应设法归还原主。如旅客已经下车，应编制客运记录，注明品名、件数等移交下车站。不能判明时，移交列车终点站。

（2）车站对本站发现或列车移交的遗失物品，应在遗失物品登记簿上详细登记，注明日期、地点、移交车次、品名、包装及内含物品、数量、重量、交物人、经办人、处理结果等内容。

（3）客流量较大的车站应设遗失物品招领处，遗失物品招领处应有明显的招领启事。对遗失物品应妥善保管，正确交付。失主来领取时，应查验身份证，核对时间、地点、车次、品名、件数、重量，确认无误后，由失主签收，并记录身份证号码。

（4）遗失物品需要通过铁路向失主所在站转送时，内附清单，物品加封填写客运记录和行李、包裹交接证，交列车行李员签收。物品在5千克以内的免费转送；超过5千克时，到站按品类补收运费。

（5）拾到现金应开具"客运运价杂费收据"（以下简称"客杂"）并上交，且在登记簿内注明"客杂"收据号码，当失主来领取时，开具退款证明书办理退款。

Key Point 4: Dealing with Lost Objects

（1）In accordance with "Railway Passenger Transportation Regulations of the People's Republic of China", the lost object shall be returned to it owner. In case the passenger has got off the train, transportation record shall be made with name and quantity to hand it over to the destination station. Or hand it to the terminal station in case the destination is not clear.

（2）Lost objects discovered at the station or transferred by the train shall be record on Lost and Found Book in detail with date, location, train number, name of object, package, item, quantity, weight, deliver person, operator, result and so on.

（3）Lost and Found Office shall be set in stations with large passenger flow with obvious sign for proper storage and accurate return. Identity of the owner of lost property shall be checked with the time, location, train number, name of the object, quantity and weight. The owner shall sign for receiving with ID card number after confirming.

（4）In case the lost object shall be transferred to the owner's stop, list shall be included in the enclosed package with transportation record, luggage and package transfer record for the signing of baggage men. Objects with weight within 5kg is transferred for free, and objects heavier than 5kg will be charged according to the nature of the object.

（5）Lost cash shall be handed in with "passenger transportation fare incidentals receipt（hereinafter referred to as passenger

（6）遗失物品中的危险物品、国家禁止或限制运输的物品、机要文件应立即移交公安机关或有关部门处理，不办理转送。

（7）鲜活、易腐物品和食品不负责保管和转送。

incidentals）" and write down the receipt number in the record book. The cash is returned to the owner with returning certificate.

（6）Dangerous or prohibited objects, confidential documents shall be handed to police department without transfer.

（7）Fresh or perishable objects will not be stored or transferred.

图 7-16 高铁列车长将乘客在列车上遗失的现金归还失主

Figure 7-16 Head of Crew in High Speed Train Returning Cash to the Owner

知识点五：客伤的处理

（1）客伤处理，应当坚持实事求是、依法依规、就近及时的原则。

（2）列车、车站发生旅客人身伤害时，站、车工作人员应当到场查看旅客受伤情况，报告列车长、站长组织救护，稳定人员情绪，维护现场秩序。

（3）发生旅客人身伤害后，列车长、站长应当及时组织现场查验，全面

Key Point 5: Dealing with Passengers' Injuries

（1）The principle of dealing with passengers' injury is to based facts and laws, with proximity and efficiency.

（2）In case of injuries in trains or station, service employees shall check the situation and report to the head of crew and chief of station for rescue, to reassure the passengers keep order on site.

（3）In case of passengers' injuries, head of crew and chief of station shall check

搜集、整理相关证据资料。检查旅客所持车票的票种、票号、发到站、车次、有效期及有效身份证件信息等，描绘现场旅客定位图，收集不少于两份同行人或见证人的证言及查验记录、现场照片、录像等其他相关证据，形成比较完整的证据链，能够证明发生的过程和原因，初步明确性质，并妥善保管。

（4）发生旅客人身伤害、需要保护现场时，应当及时采取措施保护现场，禁止与救援、调查无关的人员进入。必要时，可请求地方政府协助。

（5）当受伤旅客需交车站处理时，应移交前方县、市所在地车站或者当地具备公共医疗条件的停车站；需要提前报告运行所在铁路局客运调度时，由客运调度通知车站做好救护准备工作。

（6）旅客不同意在前款规定的停车站下车处理时，应当由旅客出具拒绝下车治疗的书面声明，并按规定收集两份及以上证人的证言。

（7）列车向车站移交受伤旅客时，车站不得拒绝接收。办理移交手续时，列车应当编制客运记录和旅客携带物品清单，一式两份，一份由列车存查，一份连同车票、证明材料、相关证人或其联系方式等一并移交。客运记录应载明日期、车次，旅客姓名、性别、年龄、国籍、民族、职业、单位、有效身份证件号码、联系方式、住址，车票种类、

the site to collect and maintain evidence; check the type and number of ticket, departure and destination station, valid period and valid ID card; portray the position map at site; collect evidence of check record, pictures of the site, video and so son from at least two witnesses to form a complete evidence chain, for a clear understand of the process and its causes; and to keep the evidence properly.

(4) In case of injuries and protection of site is necessary, protection measure is required for the entrance of only rescuers and investigators. Assistance from the local government is required if necessary.

(5) In case the injured passengers shall be treated at the station, the passengers shall be transferred to the county or municipal stations or stations with medical treatment measures; if the case shall be reported to the dispatching center in advance, the dispatching center shall inform the station for medical treatment.

(6) In case the passengers disagree to get of at the above-mentioned stations, the passengers shall give the written declaration for giving up treatment and testimonies from at least two witnesses shall be collected.

(7) The station shall not refuse to receive injured passengers. A duplicate list of transportation record and objects list shall be written in the train for storing one copy at the train and transferring one copy with ticket, proof and witness lists with contact information. Passenger transportation record shall be written with date, train number, passenger's name, gender, age, nationality, ethnic group, occupation, employer, valid ID card

号码、发站、到站、车厢、席位、受伤地点、受伤原因、受伤部位、处理简况，以及证据材料清单等内容。

（8）车站对本站发生的及列车移交的伤害旅客，应当及时联系当地医疗急救机构或送就近医院抢救。产生医疗费用时，应当根据对责任的初步判断，属于旅客自身责任或第三人责任的，由旅客或第三人支付医疗费用；暂不能区分责任或者责任人不明、无力承担的，经处理站站长或者车务段段长批准，可用站进款垫付。

（9）列车因旅客受伤严重需紧急停车处理或发生3人以上疑似食物中毒的，应立即报告运行所在铁路局客运调度。接到报告后，客运调度应当立即根据列车长提出的要求，通知有关车站及值班主任（列车调度员），需要停车处理的停车处理，并报告本铁路局客运处。

（10）受伤旅客经现场抢救无效死亡，或对站内、区间发现的旅客尸体，经医疗部门或公安机关确认死亡，公安机关现场勘查结束后，车站应当将尸体转送殡仪馆存放（在此之前，车站应将尸体转移至适当地点并派人看守），并尽快通知其家属。尸体存放原则上不超过10日。

（11）对下列情形造成的旅客人身伤害，应当立即向铁路公安机关报警：

number, contact information, address, type of ticket, number, departure and destination station, coach number, seat class, site, reason and position of injuries, treatment status, and list of evidence.

（8）Station shall contact local medical institutions or send the injured passengers to hospital. In case the passengers or a third party is responsible for the injuries, the expenses shall be borne by the passengers or the third party; in case the responsibility is not clear or the person responsible cannot afford the expenses, the station can pay it for the passengers with the revenue of the station with the consent of the chief of station or section chief.

（9）In case emergency stop is necessary or food poison of three persons or above, the case shall be reported to the dispatching center of the bureau. On receiving the report, dispatching center shall inform relevant stations and director on duty (train dispatcher) on the requirement of the head of crew. Train is stopped and the case is reported to the passenger transportation department of the bureau.

（10）In case the injured passengers die after rescue or bodies discovered in the stations and section, the death shall be confirmed by medical department or police department. And the body shall be transferred to the mortuary house by the station on the completion of the police investigation on site (the body shall be transferred to the proper location with special guard by the station before investigation), family members shall be informed as soon as possible. Body shall not be stored over 10 days in principle.

① 杀人、抢劫、抢夺、强奸、爆炸、纵火、绑架、结伙斗、寻衅滋事、意外伤害、击打列车、故意损毁、移动站车设备等违法犯罪行为；

② 因散布谣言、谎报险情、疫情、警情、扬言放火、爆炸、投放危险物质，或者非法阻拦行车、堵塞通道等，引起公共秩序混乱；

③ 火灾、爆炸、中毒等治安灾害事故；

④ 精神病人肇事肇祸，醉酒滋事行为；

⑤ 自然灾害；

⑥ 铁路设备、设施故障造成的事故。

（12）发生旅客人身伤害有下列情形之一的，应当及时通知铁路公安机关：

① 应当控制、约束违法犯罪嫌疑人和扣押相关涉案物品的；

② 应当保护现场、维持秩序、协同救助的；

③ 应当由铁路公安机关介入调查、获取证据、查明原因的；

④ 引发治安纠纷或者酿成群体性事件并影响站车秩序，应当及时处置的；

⑤ 造成旅客死亡的。

(11) In case of passenger injuries of the following situations, the case shall be reported to the railway police department:

① Murder, robbery, loot, rape, explosion, arson, kidnap, gang fighting or seeking trouble, accidental injury, slapping the train, intentional damage or moving equipment at the train station.

② Causing public chaos by demagoguery, reporting untrue dangers, epidemic or emergencies, threaten to set fire, explode, put dangerous objects; illegal stop of train, blockage of passageways.

③ Public accidents such as fire, explosion and poisoning.

④ Trouble or accident caused by psychiatric patient, causing trouble after drinking.

⑤ Natural disaster.

⑥ Accidents caused by equipment or facility failures.

(12) Any of the following passenger injuries shall be reported to railway police department:

① Suspects shall be restrained or controlled or objects related to the case shall be confiscated.

② The scene shall be protected, order to kept with coordinated assistance.

③ Train police department shall involve in investigation for evidence collecting and cause finding;

④ Public disputes or group incidents that affect the order at the station requiring instant dealing.

⑤ Cases causing death of passengers.

图 7-17　高铁乘务员将受伤乘客背下车
Figure 7-17　High Speed Train Service Employee Carrying Injured Passenger off Train

学习笔记
Study Notes

模块三　课堂练习

以小组为单位，对高铁突发事件及其处理进行模拟演练。演练前，每组从"旅客因病下车、旅客无票乘车拒绝补票、列车发现危险物品、物品遗失、客伤"中分别抽取一种需要模拟的突发事件。随后进行30分钟的情节设计及排练（设计的动作及台词写在下框），力求将抽取的突发事件及处理方法较为生动、准确地展示出来。分组模拟演练展示结束后，老师进行点评。

Module 3　In-class Exercises

Work in groups to simulate emergency handling at the high speed railway station. Every group selects randomly from the incidents of "passenger getting off due to illness, passenger without ticket rejecting compensation, discovering dangerous objects in the train, objects lost and passenger injury". Every group prepares for 30 minutes before presentation with vivid and accurate details. Teacher comments on the presentation.

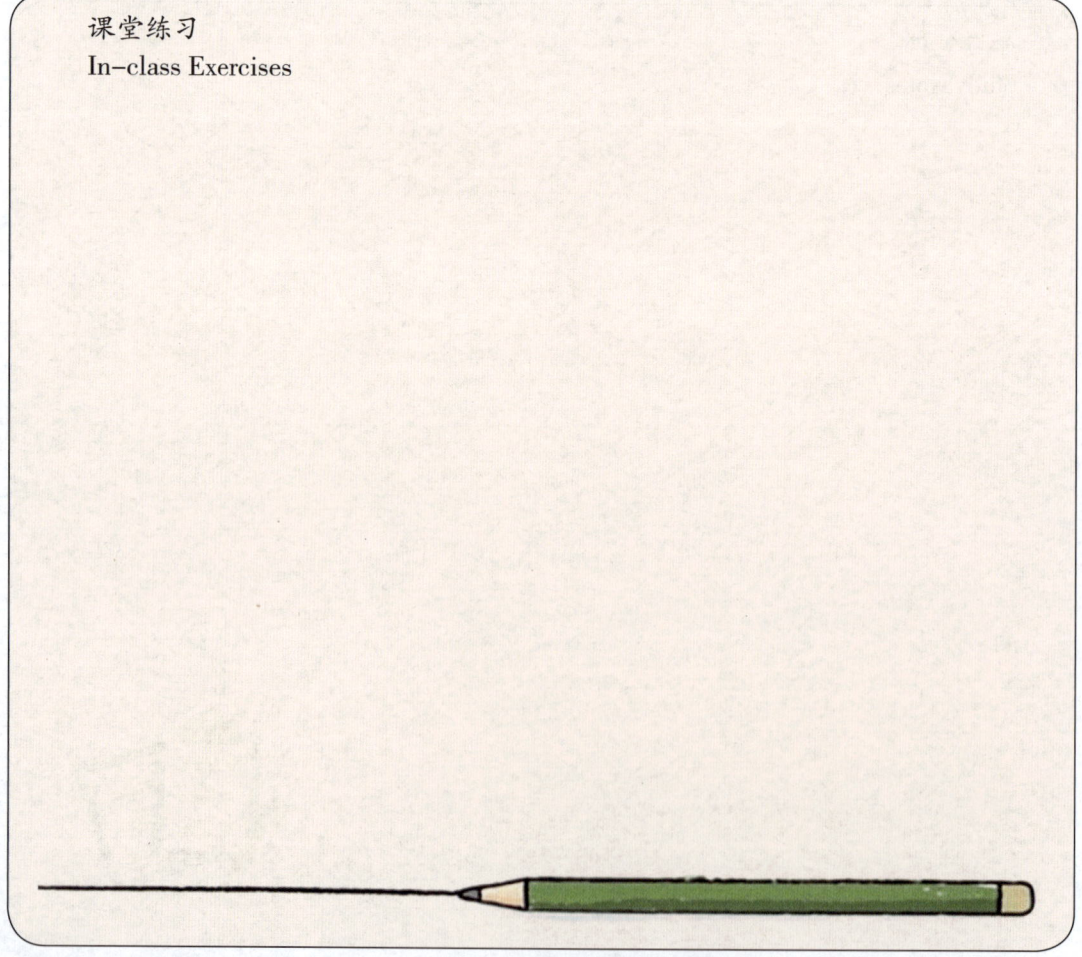

课堂练习
In-class Exercises

模块四 课后拓展

请你利用网络查询《中华人民共和国铁路旅客运输规程》，并利用在线翻译软件了解全文。写出哪些规定的内容令你印象比较深刻，并简单说明原因。

Module 4　After-class Activity

Search "Railway Passenger Transportation Regulations of the People's Republic of China" on the Internet and try to understand the content. Write down the most impressive part and explain the reasons.

After-class Activity

项目八　重点旅客服务

Project 8　Service to Special Passengers

任务一　外籍旅客服务

Task 1　Service to Foreign Passengers

模块一　学前准备

搜集中铁银通卡章程、《北京铁路局高铁快运运输管理办法》、银通卡、护照、港澳通行证、台湾居民往来大陆通行证、行李包裹、车票、餐车等动车服务相关备品。

Module 1　Preparation before Class

Search Regulaitons of China Railway Union Pay Bank card, "Beijing Railway Bureau CHR Express Transportation Management Regulations", union pay card, passport, Exit-Entry Permit for Travelling to and from Hong Kong and Macao, travelling passes for Taiwan residents to enter ot leave the mainland, luggage pack, ticket, catering coach and other relevant supplies.

课前学习笔记
Study Notes before Class

模块二 课堂学习

知识点一：银通卡的申购及购票方法

Module 2 In-class Learning

Key Point 1：Application of and Purchase with China Railway Union Pay Card

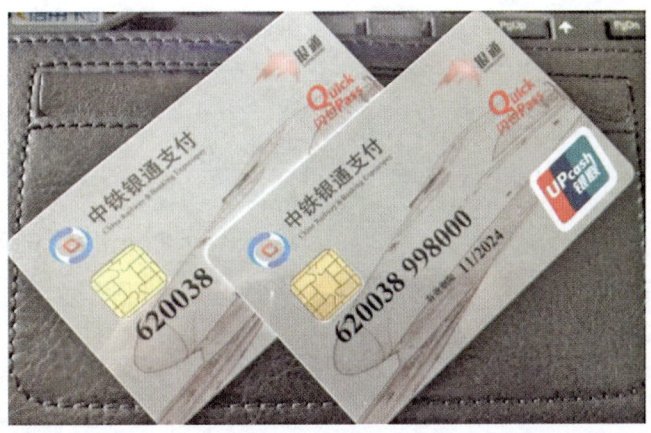

图 8-1　中铁银通卡

Figure 8-1　China Railway Union Pay Card

1. 外籍旅客申购中铁银通卡条件及手续

（1）具有完全民事行为能力的个人，可凭有效身份证件到售卡网点申购中铁银通卡。如委托他人代办，购买人须持本人及申购人有效身份证件至售卡网点办理。

（2）购卡时使用的有效身份证件范围：按规定可使用的有效护照、港澳居民来往内地通行证、台湾居民来往大陆通行证。

（3）外籍旅客购买中铁银通卡，应按规定出示有效身份证件，认真阅读并同意本章程后，填写购卡申请表，经售卡网点审核通过后可购买中铁银通卡，如图 8-1 所示。

1. Requirement and Procedures for Foreign Passengers Application for China Railway Union Pay Card

（1）Passenger with full capacity for civil conducts can apply for the card at the selling branches。Authorized representative can apply at the branches with valid ID cards of the representative and the applier.

（2）Valid ID cards for application：valid passport，Exit-Entry Permit for Travelling to and from Hong Kong and Macao，travelling passes for Taiwan residents to enter ot leave the mainland.

（3）After reading and consenting the regulations carefully, foreign passengers shall offer valid ID cards and fill application form for the verification of the branch to purchase the union pay card; as illustrated in Figure 8-1.

2. 外籍旅客使用银通卡购票的方法

（1）铁路安装有POS机的售票窗口。

（2）支持银行卡支付的自助售票机。

（3）中国铁路客户服务中心网站（www.12306.cn）等渠道。

（4）中铁银通卡刷卡乘车。

知识点二：国境站手续办理内容

（1）礼貌地欢迎旅客，热情、耐心地回答旅客的询问，使用礼貌用语，为国际列车旅客提供快速、专业、人性化的服务，确保安检工作的快速进行。

（2）帮助国际列车旅客办理海关手续。

（3）回答旅客关于国际列车车票的询问。

（4）用英语向乘客解释相关的铁路法规。

2. Ways for Foreign Passengers Buying Ticket with the Union Pay Card

(1) Ticket selling windows with POS terminals.

(2) Automatic ticket selling machine accessible for bank card.

(3) www.12306.cn and other ways.

(4) Taking trains by using the union pay card.

Key Point 2: Procedures at the Border Stations

(1) Welcome passengers politely, answer questions with enthusiasm, patience and courtesy, serving passengers in international trains with fast, specialized and personalized service to ensure smooth safety check.

(2) Help passengers with customs procedures.

(3) Answer passengers' questions about international tickets.

(4) Explain railway rules and regulations to passengers in English.

图 8-2　北京—莫斯科 K3/4 次国际列车国境站

Figure 8-2　Border Station of K3/4 International Train from Beijing to Moscow

知识点三：高铁列车英语服务

随着我国国际化水平的不断提高，高铁作为对外服务窗口，对乘务人员的英语服务能力也有了更高的要求。通过一些实用性练习，循序渐进提升客运服务英语会话水平，为外籍旅客提供更加优质的服务，如图8-3所示。

Key Point 3：English Service in High Speed Trains

High speed train is the window to the international community, and requirement of English language levels for the service employees is getting higher. English conversation ability can be improved gradually through practical training to provide foreign passengers with quality service; as illustrated in Figure 8-3.

图8-3 高铁英语服务

Figure 8-3 English Service in the High Speed Train

（实训案例检票上车）

（1）请出示您的车票。

（2）谢谢，欢迎您乘车。

（3）请问，我可以提前多长时间上车？

（4）您可以在火车出发前××分钟上车。

（5）非常抱歉，我们不清楚晚点的原因，一有任何消息，我们会通知大家。

（6）请拿出车票来剪票。

（7）请将车票准备好。

（8）乘坐G12次列车的旅客，请到

（Boarding the Train）

（1）Show me your ticket, please!

（2）Thank you, welcome aboard.

（3）How long can I get on board before train departure, please?

（4）You may get on board x x minutes before the train leaves.

（5）We are very sorry that we do not know the reason for delay, and we will inform you if there is any news.

（6）Take your tickets out for punching, please.

（7）Please get your tickets ready.

（8）Passengers for Train G12, please go to the boarding gate and get ready for

检票口准备上车。

（9）开始检票时，工作人员将会通知您。

（10）列车开车前30分钟开始检票，请稍等一会儿。

（11）现在您的车票已经剪了，请收好，小心慢走。

（12）您的车票是昨天的，但已经失效了。

（13）请给您的女儿买张儿童票。

（14）女士们、先生们，请注意。本站开往上海的G11次列车开始检票上车了。乘坐这趟列车的旅客们，请准备好车票，前往2号检票口。请旅客们确认没有把任何东西遗忘在候车室，谢谢。

（15）旅客们请注意，由本站开往南京的G55次列车开始检票上车了。乘坐这趟列车的旅客请前往5号检票口，谢谢。

boarding.

（9）Staff will inform you when ticket checking begins.

（10）Ticket checking starts 30 minutes before the train leaves. Wait a moment, please.

（11）Now your ticket is punched. Keep it, please and be careful.

（12）Your ticket was valid for yesterday's train, but it's no longer valid.

（13）Please buy a child-ticket for your daughter.

（14）Ladies and gentlemen, attention, please. The station announces the boarding of Express Train G11 for Shanghai. Passengers for this train, please get your tickets ready and go to Boarding Gate 2. You are advised to make sure that you've nothing left behind in the waiting room. Thank you.

（15）Attention, please. The station announces the boarding of Express Train G55 for Nanjing. Passengers for this train please go to Boarding Gate 5. Thank you.

学习笔记
Study Notes

模块三 课堂练习

（1）分小组及角色练习中铁银通卡的申购及购票方法。

（2）分小组及角色模拟国境站手续办理（包括出境检票、出入境行李托运与提取等情景）。

（3）分小组及角色模拟外籍乘客检票上车常用英语。

Module 3 In-class Exercises

（1）Role play practice of application for and buying ticket with China railway union pay card in groups.

（2）Role play practice of procedures at the border train stations in groups （check in to go abroad, luggage check-in and claim at entry and exit point.）

（3）Practice the English language used by foreign passengers during check-in in groups.

课堂练习
In-class Exercises

模块四　课后拓展

在高铁列车运行过程中，客运员发现有外籍乘客在卫生间里抽烟，此时作为客运服务员你该如何做？

Module 4　After-class Activity

As a train attendant, how do you deal with the situation when a foreign passenger is discovered smoking in the lavatory in the process of train running?

After-class Activity

任务二 重点旅客服务

Task 2　Service to Special Passengers

模块一　学前准备

Module 1　Preparation before Class

提前准备动车组列车服务质量规范、客运车间重点旅客服务流程（〔2015〕7号）、乘务人员对讲机、爱心送站卡、担架、轮椅、《重点旅客登记簿》、《特殊重点旅客服务交接簿》、手持终端等动车组重点旅客服务相关备品。

Prepare CHR train service quality standard, service procedure for special passengers (〔2015〕No. 7), walkie-talkie, warm-hearted sending card, stretcher, wheelchair, "Special Passenger Registration Book", "Handover Registration Book for Special Passenger Service", portable terminal and other equipment for special passenger service.

课前学习笔记
Study Notes before Class

模块二　课堂学习

知识点一：一般重点旅客服务

（1）一般重点旅客：指老、幼、病、残、孕且有同行人陪同的旅客，或无须工作人员全程护送，需车站提供优先服务的旅客。

（2）一般重点旅客服务流程如图8-4所示。

Module 2　In-class Learning

Key Point 1: Service to Ordinary Special Passengers

（1）Ordinary special passengers are the old, young, ill, disabled and pregnant passengers with fellow travelers, or those not requiring the companion and boarding service of the service employees.

（2）Service procedure for ordinary special passengers is as illustrated in Figure 8-4.

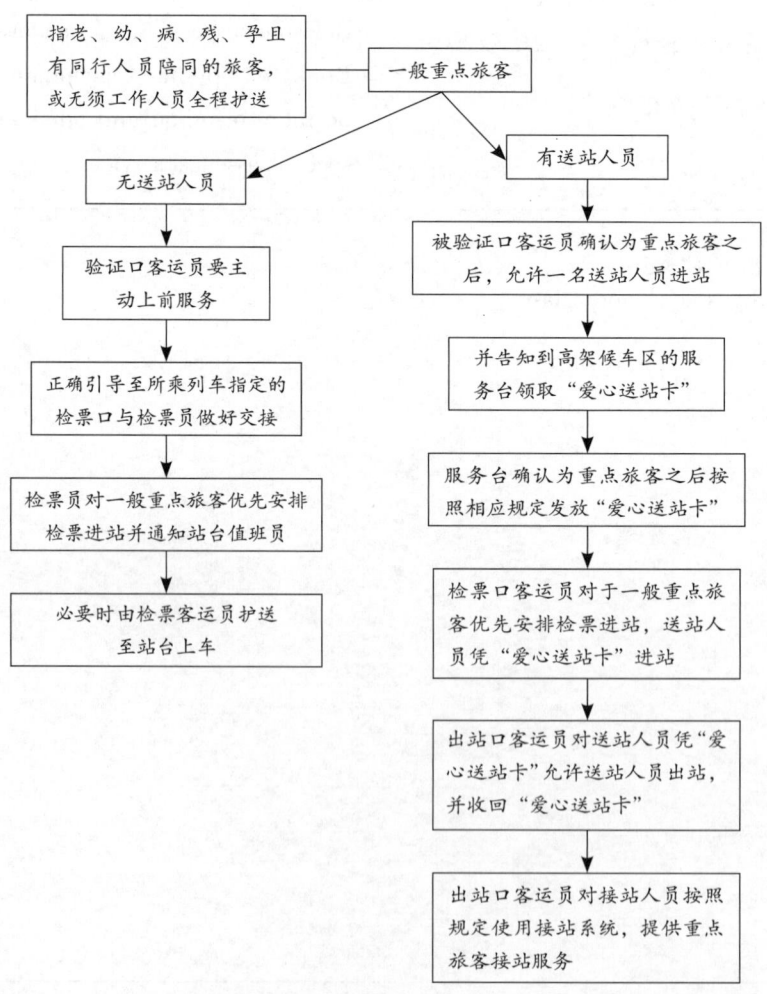

一般重点旅客：ordinary special passengers

指老、幼、病、残、孕且有同行人员陪同的旅客，或无须工作人员全程护送：
old, young, ill, disabled and pregnant passengers with fellow traveller, or not requiring accompany of employees;

无送站人员：without seeing-off companions

验证口客运员要主动上前服务：service employee at the check point serves actively

正确引导至所乘列车指定的检票口与检票员做好交接：
guiding the passenger to the check-in gate and hand over with the check-in employee

检票员对一般重点旅客优先安排检票进站并通知站台值班员：
check-in employee arrange for the special passengers with priority and inform the employee on the platform

必要时由检票客运员护送至站台上车：
check-in employee can send the passengers to the platform if necessary

有送站人员：with seeing-off companions

被验证口客运员确认为重点旅客之后，允许一名送站人员进站：
employee at the check point permits one companion to enter after confirmation

并告知到高架候车区的服务台领取"爱心送站卡"：
tell them to get warm-hearted sending card at the reception desk in the waiting area

服务台确认为重点旅客之后按照相应规定发放"爱心送站卡"：
getting warm-hearted sending card at the reception desk after confirmation

检票口客运员对于一般重点旅客优先安排检票进站，送站人员凭"爱心送站卡"进站：
check-in employee arrange for the passenger with priority and the sending companion enters with the card

出站口客运员对送站人员凭"爱心送站卡"允许送站人员出站，并收回"爱心送站卡"：
the sending companion exits with the card and give the card back

出站口客运员对接站人员按照规定使用接站系统，提供重点旅客接站服务：
passenger receiving system is used by employee at the exit for the passenger meeting person and provide receiving service for special passengers

图 8-4　一般重点旅客服务流程

Figure 8-4　Ordinary Special Passengers

知识点二：特殊旅客服务流程

Key Point 2: Service Procedure to Special Passengers

特殊重点旅客是指盲人和靠辅助器具如担架、轮椅行动的旅客，需要工作人员特殊照顾或者全程护送的旅客。铁路对于特殊重点旅客的服务流程如图8-5所示。

Extraordinarily special passengers are the blind passengers or those rely on auxiliary tools such as stretchers and wheelchairs, requiring special care and accompany. The service procedure is illustrated in Figure 8-5.

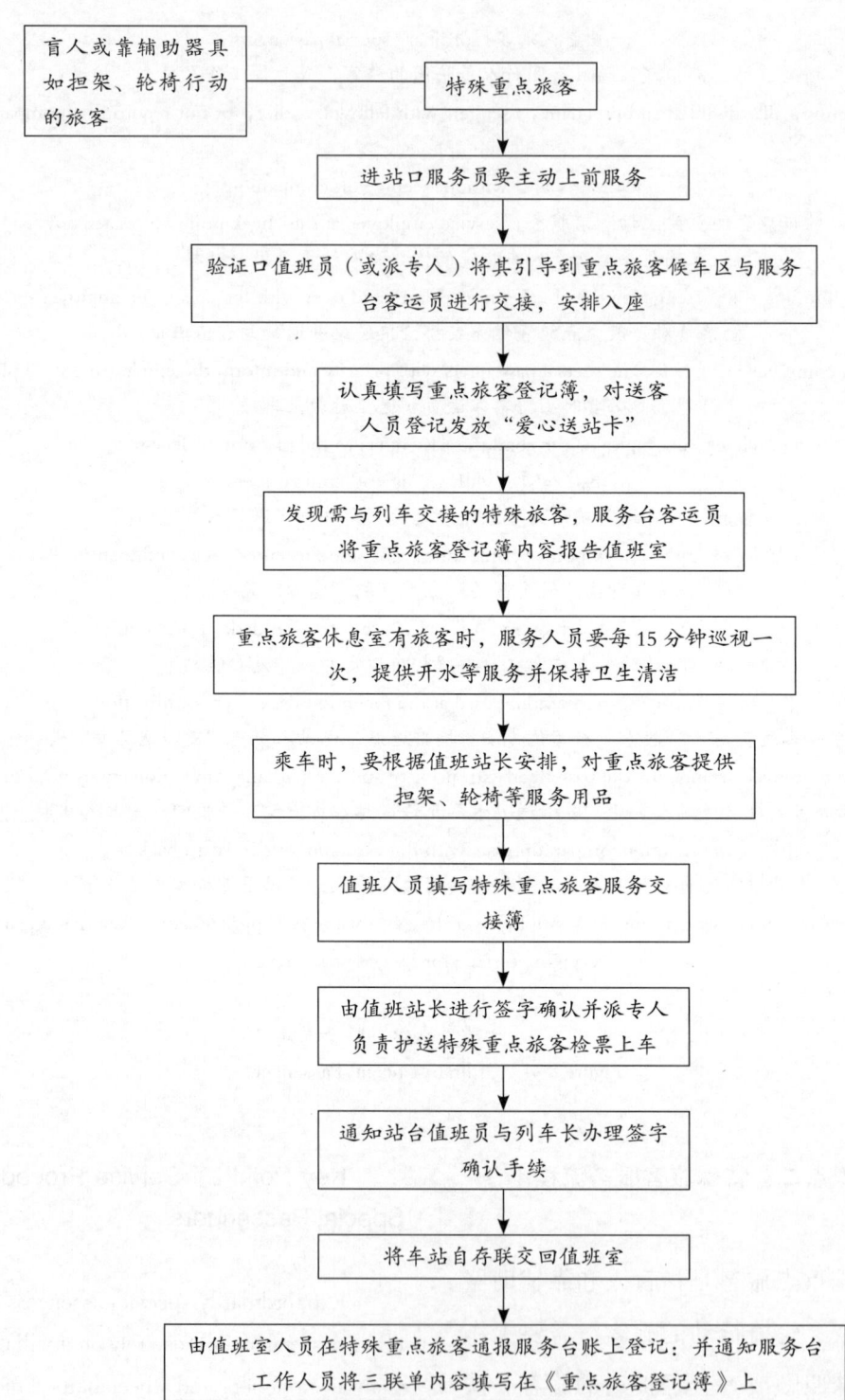

特殊重点旅客：extraordinary special passengers
盲人或靠辅助器具如担架、轮椅行动的旅客：
the blind or those relying on auxiliary tools such as stretchers or wheelchair

进站口服务员要主动上前服务：service employee at the entrance shall offer help actively

验证口值班员（或派专人）将其引导到重点旅客候车区与服务台客运员进行交接，安排入座：employee on duty at the check point（or a specially-assigned person）guide the passenger to the special waiting area and handover with the passenger service employee at the reception for seat arrangement

认真填写重点旅客登记簿，对送客人员登记发放"爱心送站卡"：fill in special passenger registration book and give warm-hearted sending card to the sending companion

发现需与列车交接的特殊旅客，服务台客运员将重点旅客登记簿内容报告值班室：report the registration content to the duty room if the special passenger shall be handed over with the train

重点旅客休息室有旅客时，服务人员要每15分钟巡视一次，提供开水等服务并保持卫生清洁：service employee shall tour the waiting room every 15 minutes if there are special passengers, provide hot drinking water or other service, and keep the waiting room clean

乘车时，要根据值班站长安排，对重点旅客提供担架、轮椅等服务用品：chief of station on duty shall serve the special passengers with stretcher, wheelchairs in taking the train

值班人员填写特殊重点旅客服务交接簿：employee on duty fill in special passenger service handover registration

由值班站长进行签字确认并派专人负责护送特殊重点旅客检票上车：send special passenger on board with specially assigned person with the written confirmation of the chief of station on duty

通知站台值班员与列车长办理签字确认手续：inform platform employee on duty to sign and confirm with head of crew

将车站自存联交回值班室：take a signing copy back to the station on duty

由值班室人员在特殊重点旅客通报服务台账上登记，并通知服务台工作人员将三联单内容填写在《重点旅客登记簿》上：employee on duty write the special passenger service on the record and inform the employee at the reception desk to fill the triplicate on "Special Passenger Registration Book"

图 8-5 特殊重点旅客服务流程

Figure 8-5　Service Procedure for Extraordinary Special Passengers

知识点三：12306 预约的重点旅客服务

一些老、弱、病、残、幼、孕重点旅客乘坐火车的时候需要提前预约，否则将和普通旅客一同进站，这样很容易发生危险，需提前预约进站。车站对通过 12306 预约的重点旅客服务流程图如图 8-6 所示。

Key Point 3: Special Passenger Service Reserved on 12306.cn

Entering service of some special passengers can be reserved in advance to avoid the possible dangers occurring when entering with ordinary passengers. Reservation procedure on 12306.cn is illustrated in Figure 8-6.

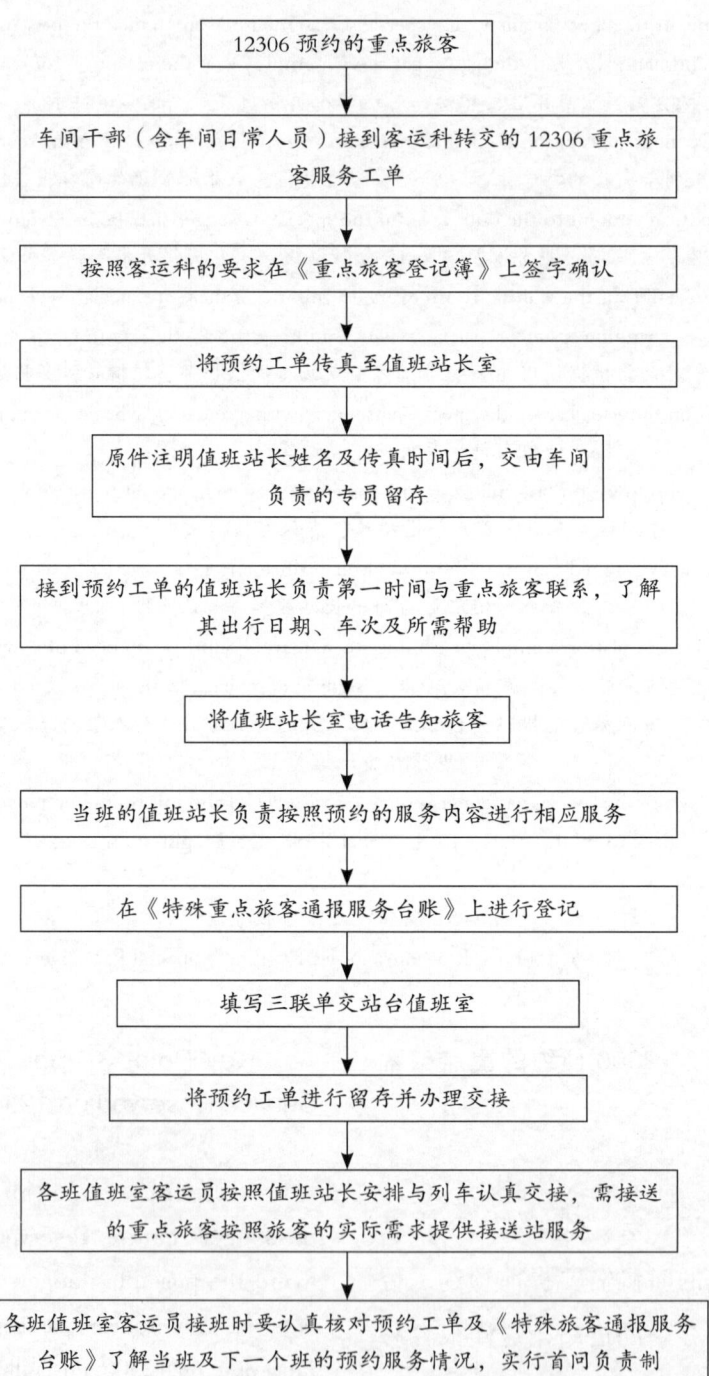

12306 预约的重点旅客：special passengers reserved on 12306. cn

车间干部（含车间日常人员）接到客运科转交的 12306 重点旅客服务工单： leaders and employees receiving 12306 special passenger service work order transferred by passenger transportation department

按照客运科的要求在《重点旅客登记簿》上签字确认： sign and confirm in "Special Passenger Registration Book" according to the requirement of the passenger transportation department

将预约工单传真至值班站长室：fax the work order to the station duty office

原件注明值班站长姓名及传真时间后，交由车间负责的专员留存： write name of the chief of station on duty and time of fax on the original work order and hand it to the specialized employee for storing

接到预约工单的值班站长负责第一时间与重点旅客联系，了解其出行日期、车次及所需帮助： chief of station contact with the special passenger on receiving the work order to know the date, train number and the help needed

将值班站长室电话告知旅客：inform the passenger of the telephone number of the duty office

当班的值班站长负责按照预约的服务内容进行相应服务：chief of station on duty serves as required

在《特殊重点旅客通报服务台账》上进行登记：fill in "Extraordinary Special Passenger Service Record"

填写三联单交站台值班室：hand the triplicate record to the duty office

将预约工单进行留存并办理交接：store the reservation order and hand over

各班值班室客运员按照值班站长安排与列车认真交接，需接送的重点旅客按照旅客的实际需求提供接送站服务： passenger service employee hands over and serve the special passengers as required

各班值班室客运员接班时要认真核对预约工单及《特殊旅客通报服务台账》了解当班及下一个班的预约服务情况，实行首问负责制： employee on duty shall check the reservation order and "Extraordinary Special Passenger Service Record" to know the service status of the current and next shift with first inquiry accountability system

图 8-6　12306 预约重点旅客服务流程

Figure 8-6　Procedure for Special Passenger Service Reservation

学习笔记
Study Notes

模块三　课堂练习

（1）分小组及角色模拟老年旅客、儿童旅客、患病旅客、残疾旅客、孕妇旅客等一般重点旅客服务流程。

（2）分小组及角色模拟盲人等特殊重点旅客服务流程。

Module 3　In-class Exercises

（1）Simulate service procedures for old, children, ill, disabled and pregnant passengers in groups.

（2）Simulate service procedures for blind and other extraordinary special passengers in groups.

课堂练习
In-class Exercises

模块四　课后拓展

练习《特殊重点旅客服务交接簿》的填写，如图 8-7 所示。

Module 4　After-class Activity

Practice filling of "Extraordinary Special Passenger Service Handover Record", as illustrated in Figure 8-7.

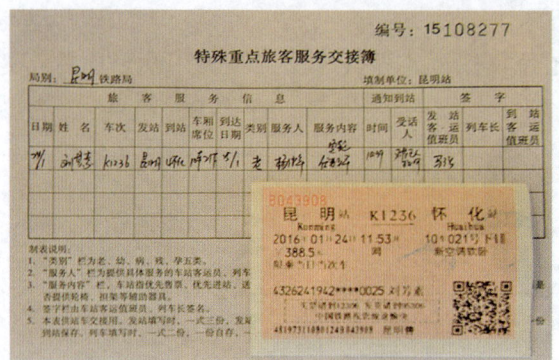

图 8-7　《特殊重点旅客服务交接簿》（图片来自央广网）

Figure 8-7　Extraordinary Special Passenger Service Handover Record（picture from cnr. cn）

课后拓展

After-class Activity

任务三 列车接待工作

Task 3　Reception in the Train

模块一　学前准备

搜集列车长接待工作指导等动车组服务相关备品。

Module 1　Preparation before Class

Collect information on the equipment required for CHR train reception by the head of crew.

　课前学习笔记
Study Notes before Class

模块二　课堂学习

知识点一：接待对象及汇报工作内容

Module 2　In-class Learning

Key Point 1：Reception and Work Report

图 8-8　接待对象

Figure 8-8　Reception

（1）重要领导乘车时，应事先与秘书或陪同人员取得联系，确定汇报人员和汇报时间。一般领导也要先请示再汇报。

（2）汇报工作一般在餐车或包房内进行，汇报前要整理好衣帽及佩戴的标志，带好本和笔，进包房时要先敲门，待得到允许后再开门进入。

（3）进包房后首先向主要领导敬礼，然后由左至右依次敬礼（遇领导先伸手握手时，再握手，不要主动和领导握手），待领导示意坐下时，要靠包房门口一边面向主要领导堂下（不要吸烟、跷腿），汇报时力求平稳从容，简明扼要，吐字清楚，实事求是。讲话速度不

（1）Person and time of report shall be confirmed with the secretary or accompanying leaders in advance in case important leaders taking trains. Report to ordinary leader shall be done after receiving instructions.

（2）Report is usually done in the catering coach or compartment after checking dress and signs with notebook and pens; entering the compartment with permission.

（3）Salute leaders in the compartment first and salute to people from left to right (don't shake hands first, shake hands after the leader stretches for handshaking); sit by the door toward the major leader (don't smoke or cross legs). Report the facts precisely and clearly. Don't speak too fast with the duration of report of 10-20 minutes. Leave the compartment in moving back

要太快，汇报时间掌握在10~20分钟。汇报完毕出包房时要退行。

（4）遇兄弟单位领导乘车汇报时，不要随意告状、中伤，让领导察觉工作中的不协调和不团结。要策略、婉转地倾诉工作中的难处，争取得到理解和支持。

（5）对领导提出的问题和指示，要做好记录（不要用纸和不规矩的笔记本）。提出批评时，不要强调客观，不要进行申辩，要态度诚恳地表示立即改正或落实。

（6）汇报材料最好准备两套，一套是书面语言，正规迎检时用；一套是口头语，平时使用。

另外对车班人员状况、车体设备状况等一定要熟知。

知识点二：接待工作程序

1. 接待工作中的握手方式

握手方式：怎样握手、伸手次序由尊者决定。公务场合，职务高、身份高者先伸手；非公务场合，年长者、女性先伸手。握手动作双目注视对方，面带微笑。对方伸手后，我方应迅速迎上去，身体稍前倾，伸出右手，手掌与地面平行，四指并拢，拇指张开，持续3~6秒。初次见面一般3秒以内，如图8-9所示。

position.

(4) Don't slaughter or complain to the leaders of fellow institutions to make the discordance or disunity perceived by the leaders. Understanding and support can be gained through telling difficulties in the work tactfully.

(5) Write down questions and instructions of the leader (don't use paper or improper notebook). Don't argue against criticism, determined to correct the error or carry out the instructions.

(6) Prepare two copies of document for report; one written and formal copy for report; and one oral copy for daily use.

Good command of the status of crew and equipment.

Key Point 2: Reception Procedure

1. Handshaking Manner in Reception

Handshaking manner: manner and order of handshaking is determined by social status. Person with higher rank and social status reaches out first in formal occasion; the elder and female reaches out first in informal occasion. Shaking hands with both eyes looking at the other person with smile. When the other person reaches out, walking forward and reaching out with right hand with the palm parallel with the ground, thumb stretching out and the other four fingers folded, shaking hands for 3-6 seconds. Handshake in the first meeting lasts within 3 seconds. As illustrated in Figure 8-9.

图 8-9　接待工作握手

Figure 8-9　Handshake in Reception

2. 接待工作中的致意方式

致意方式：微笑、点头、指手、欠身、鞠躬、脱帽等。基本规范：男士首先向女士致意，年轻者先向年长者致意，下级应当首先向上级致意，当年轻的女士遇到比自己年岁大得多的男士的时候，应首先向男士致意（如图 8-10 所示）。

2. Greeting Manners in Reception

Greeting manners: smile, nodding, hand pointing, raising body slightly, bow, taking off hats and so on. Basic rules: men greet ladies first, young people greet to the elder first, juniors greet seniors first, young lady greets older men first. As illustrated in Figure 8-10.

图 8-10　致意方式

Figure 8-10　Greeting Manners

3. 接待工作中用餐的注意事项

接待用餐的内容：预先把用餐的时间、地点告知客人和陪同的领导；掌握用餐的人数、用餐方式和标准，并提前

3. Dinning Manners in Reception

Content of reception dinning: inform guests and leaders of the time and location of dinning; command the number of person, type and standard of dinning and inform head

通知餐车长。厨师长做好用餐设计，编制用餐菜单。提前1小时到餐厅，督促检查有关服务。做好引导和服务。

用餐桌次排列：主桌位置，圆厅居中为上，横排以右为上，纵排以远为上（指的是距高门的位置），有讲台时临台为上。其他以离主桌位置的远近确定，近高远低，右高左低（桌数较多时，要摆桌次牌、通常安排每桌10人）。

用餐座次排列：只有一位主人时，1号来宾坐在主人右侧，2号来宾坐在主人左侧，其余人员依次就座。当有两位主人时，1号来宾坐在第一主人的右侧，2号来宾坐在第一主人的左侧，3号来宾坐在第二主人右侧，4号来宾坐在第二主人左侧，其他来宾依次就座，如图8-11所示。

of the catering coach. Chef designs the dinner and prepares menu. Arrive at the dinning hall 1 hour in advance for supervision and check. Prepare for guiding and service.

Order of tables: the main table is in the center of the round hall, the right of the horizontal line, and the farthest place from the door in straight line. Other tables is arranged in the order of near to the far place and right to the left from the main table (table number is set if there are various table, and the number of guests in each table is around 10).

Dinning seat arrangement: if there is only one host, number one guest sits on the right of the host and number two guest sits on the left of the host and other guests sit in order. If there are two guests, number one guest sits on the right of the first guest, number two guest sits on the left of the first host, number three guest sits on the right of the second host, number four guest sits on the left of the second host and other guests sit in order. As illustrated in Figure 8-11.

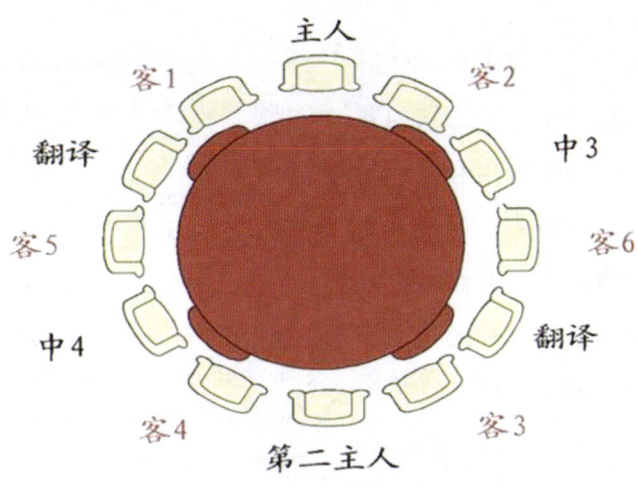

图8-11　接待工作用餐礼仪

Figure 8-11　Reception Dinning Manners

4. 接待工作中各种座次的排列原则

合影座次排定：周前为上、居中为上、周左为上。与来宾合影时一般由主人居中，主人右侧为上；两端均由主方人员把边。如主要领导居中，通常排单数就座，2 号人员在领导左侧，3 号人员在领导右侧；如图 8-12 所示。

4. Seat Order Arrangement Principles in Reception

Group photo position arrangement: the major position is in the front, middle and left. Host is usually in the middle of guests and the important position is on the right of the host; people from the organizing party are on the both sides. If the major leader is in the middle, seats are arranged in lines of odd number. Number two person is on the left of the leader and number three person is on the right of the leader. As illustrated in Figure 8-12.

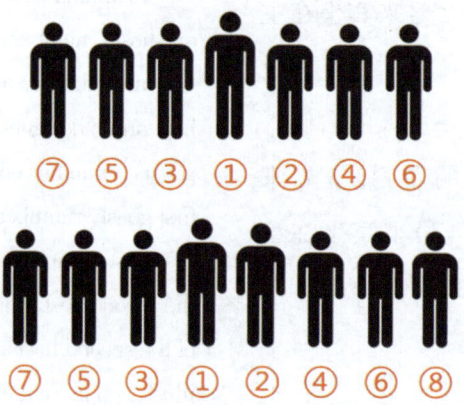

图 8-12 合影座次排定

Figure 8-12　Group Photo Position Arrangement

乘车位置的排序：注意上车时让客人和领导先上，自己后上。要主动为客人和来宾打开车门。乘坐轿车有专职司机开车时，司机的右后方为上座，其次是正后方。如果是主人自己开车，主人的右侧（副驾驶）为上座。乘坐中大型面包车时，司机后边的第一排右侧临窗的位置为上座。其他位置，前座高于后座，右座高于左座；距离前门越近，座次越高。

Car taking position arrangement: guest and leader gets in the car first, open the door for guests. If the car if driven by a chauffeur, the best seat is the right seat in the back of the driving seat and the next one is the middle seat in the back. If the host drives the car, the best seat is the right seat beside the driver. In taking medium-sized van, the right seat beside the window in the first row beside the driver is the best one. And for other seats, the front seats on the right side are better.

观看节目的座次安排：一般以第七排、第八排座位居中为最佳，观看电影则是第十五排前后居中为最佳。专场演出时要把最佳席位留给主人和主要客人，其他客人可排座位，也可自由入座。

Seat arrangement in watching performance: middle seats in row seven and eight are the best seats; best seats in watching movie are the middle seats in row 15; the best seats shall be reserved for host and important guest, other guests can select from the arranged seats or choose seats by themselves.

学习笔记
Study Notes

模块三　课堂练习

（1）若上级领导到车站视察工作，如何接待？分小组和角色进行演练。

（2）练习接待用餐座次排序。

Module 3　In-class Exercises

（1）How to arrange reception for leaders inspection visit of the station? Role play in groups.

（2）Practice seats arrangement of reception dinner.

课堂练习
In-class Exercises

模块四 课后拓展

Module 4 After-class Activity

查询相关资料，熟悉职场其他接待工作礼仪。

Search relevant information to get a better understanding of other reception manners in work.

After-class Activity

参考文献

Reference

[1] 蓝志江, 雷莲桂. 高速铁路乘务工作实务 [M]. 北京: 北京交通大学出版社, 2015.

[2] 闫莹娜. 高速铁路客运乘务实训教程 [M]. 成都: 西南交通大学出版社, 2017.

[3] 马海漫, 宋玉佳. 高速铁路客运组织 [M]. 成都: 西南交通大学出版社, 2015.

[4] 兰云飞, 何萍. 高速铁路客运组织 [M]. 北京: 北京交通大学出版社, 2017.

[5] 张英姿. 高速铁路客运服务礼仪 [M]. 北京: 北京交通大学出版社, 2017.

[6] 潘自影. 高速铁路客运服务与礼仪 [M]. 成都: 西南交通大学出版社, 2015.

[1] Lan Zhijiang, Lei Guilian. High Speed Railway Passenger Service Practice [M]. Beijing: Beijing Jiaotong University Press, 2015.

[2] Yan Yingna, High Speed Railway Passenger Transportation Service Training Course. [M]. Chengdu: Southwest Jiaotong University Press, 2017.

[3] Ma Haiman, Song Yujia. High Speed Railway Passenger Transportation Organization. [M]. Chengdu: Southwest Jiaotong University Press, 2015.

[4] Lan Yunfei, He Ping. High Speed Railway Passenger Transportation Organization. [M]. Beijing: Beijing Jiaotong University Press, 2017.

[5] Zhang Yingzi. High Speed Railway Passenger Service Etiquette. [M]. Beijing: Beijing Jiaotong University Press, 2017.

[6] Pan Ziying. High Speed Railway Passenger Service and Etiquette. [M]. Chengdu: Southwest Jiaotong University Press, 2015.